fashion in
Underwear

from Babylon to Bikini Briefs

Elizabeth Ewing

With Illustrations by Jean Webber

DOVER PUBLICATIONS, INC.
Mineola, New York

Bibliographical Note

This Dover edition, first published in 2010, is an unabridged republication of
the work originally published by B. T. Batsford, Ltd., London, in 1971.

Library of Congress Cataloging-in-Publication Data

Ewing, Elizabeth.
    Fashion in underwear: from babylon to bikini briefs / Elizabeth Ewing
with illustrations by Jean Webber.
        p. cm.
    Originally published: New York : Batsford, [1971].
    Includes bibliographical references and index.
    ISBN-13: 978-0-486-47649-0
    ISBN-10: 0-486-47649-9
     1. Underwear. I. Title.

GT2073.E9 2010
391.4'2—dc22

                                                           2009048201

Manufactured in the United States by Courier Corporation
47649901
www.doverpublications.com

To David, Nicola, Piers and Francis

Contents

Acknowledgments

For valuable assistance in supplying and verifying information and giving access to collections of historical underwear, records and catalogues grateful thanks are due to Barbara Bristow of Aertex; Betty Williams of Berlei; L. W. Coulson of the Department of Prints and Drawings, The British Museum; Roger Parker, Editor of *Corsetry and Underwear*; Jane Hurren of Debenham & Freebody; Margrit Shaw of Du Pont (United Kingdom); Kay Staniland of the Gallery of English Costume, Manchester; Clare Donovan of Jaeger; Eric Lewis of Marks & Spencer; Rosemary James of Marshall & Snelgrove; Myra Mines of the Museum of Costume, Bath; David Quartley of Singer; Meriel McCooey of the *Sunday Times Magazine*; C. E. Page of Symington Foundationwear, and Ann Hart of the Victoria & Albert Museum. Also to Pauline Baldwin, who read the MS and made many useful comments, and Eileen Moss, who typed it and helped with the proof reading.

1 | *A Late Start:* *3000 BC – 1350 AD*

When Christian Dior, king of couture in the years after the 1939–45 war, said: 'Without foundations there can be no fashion', he could equally aptly have reversed the statement to: 'Without fashion there can be no foundations.' Fashion is a shape, a changing shape, and that shape is mainly, and sometimes even wholly, formed and controlled by what is worn underneath it, by the corset and other underwear.

These underpinnings, so many and so varied, sometimes ephemeral but more often with a long and continuous history of their own, have at times started as outerwear and gone underneath, usually because of their becoming more functional. On other occasions underwear, concealed or glimpsed for long periods, has emerged as outerwear. But in general it has its own story. That story, and the story of outer fashion, have for many centuries past been inseparable. Underwear existed in some form before fashion began, but it did not acquire any significance or any history until the dawn of fashion.

It might be assumed and is often accepted that the story of clothes and the story of fashion are contemporaneous, but this is not so. Fashion in clothes is a freak among the arts in that its existence as we understand it is limited to the Western world and to the period from the later Middle Ages onwards. Mankind has for innumerable centuries been drawing, painting, carving and sculpting, building, telling stories, dancing, singing songs and making music—in all sorts of ways such as these expressing himself and adjusting himself to the world around him by that exercise and projection of his feelings, thoughts and aspirations which we define in general as the arts.

But while these arts were continually changing and developing and taking on different forms from one era and one part of the world to another, men and women continued to dress in very much the same way generation after generation, century after century, even in one civilisation after another.

The history of clothing is usually, and reasonably, regarded by

Straight-falling Egyptian tunic, starting below waist, with crossed shoulder band and knotted sash. About 1125 BC

T-shaped tunic from Egypt c.1500 BC

most people as dating from the time when mankind discovered how to spin and weave and therefore how to make fabrics that were durable and washable. This was many thousands of years ago, and the materials used were wool, flax or cotton, according to the part of the world concerned. In China from early days it was silk, whose process of manufacture was until only a few centuries ago cherished as a closely-guarded secret by that country.

It is impossible to say for certain which clothing material came first and from where, or how the method was first discovered of how to twist the raw materials together so as to produce continuous threads from which cloth could be woven by criss-crossing them at right angles on an elementary loom. But having produced lengths of fabric, people, men and women alike, draped them round their bodies in various ways and went on doing so.

The first continuous record of such clothes came from ancient Egypt from about 3000 BC, where, as would be expected, there was a considerable degree of sophistication in the draping. Sometimes we find narrow tunics, starting below the chest, extending to the ankles and often supported by a crosswise shoulder strap. Sometimes the drapery was drawn round the figure to the front, so as to mould it, and often a short semi-circular shoulder cape was also worn. So were loin cloths. In general, clothing was a status symbol: the higher the rank the more elaborate the clothing, while slaves and servants went naked or simply wore loin cloths. But there is no evidence of basic changes in style: the same way of dressing remained. On the other hand there was immense diversity and infinite dazzling elaboration in jewellery, accessories and all kinds of adornments, as every collection of Egyptian antiquities shows.

Sometimes in Egypt there was more than one layer of clothing, one opaque and one transparent. In this case the top one was transparent, but neither could be designated as being an under-garment as we understand the word. As a variation, the clothing material, instead of simply being draped, was folded in two vertically, with a hole or slit at the top for the head, so that it became more like a tunic. Pieces were also cut out of it down the sides, forming a letter 'T' and creating wide or narrow sleeves.

This pattern of dress was to be continued and repeated, with variations in the ways of folding and draping, through subsequent eras, including both Greek and Roman civilisations. It persists to this day in many parts of the world, notably in Indian saris, Arab and other Oriental robes, and can also be seen in the context of Chinese dress and the Japanese kimono. There was nothing of recognisable fashion in it in the modern sense. There was no basic distinction between what men and women wore or between outer-wear and underwear.

Strangely, however, from this early era there remain a few female terra cotta figures and figurines of two types separated from each other by about a thousand years of history and many hundreds of miles, but standing out from the mists of time as a starting point for underclothing and, in one type, specifically women's under-clothing.

One outstanding example of the first type of figures is a Babylon-ian girl of about 3000 BC from Sumeria who wears what today would immediately be described as briefs. The other type comes from Crete, and is attired in the first recorded corset and crinoline. Her place in history is about 2000 BC. Both are unconcernedly bare-breasted and dressed in what in their day was obviously outerwear. An example of the first type can be seen in the Louvre, and of the other in the British Museum.

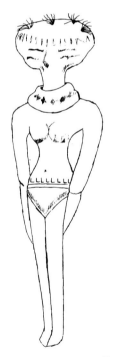

*Sumerian terra cotta figure
c.3000 BC*

*Cretan snake goddess
c.2000 BC*

Cretan woman c.2000 BC

The briefs probably derived from the loin cloth, the most elementary of early and primitive garments for both sexes and one familiar in immensely scattered parts of the world from days as remote as those of cave drawings. Draw it up between the legs it becomes crude briefs, as is shown by other figures in bas reliefs and vase drawings from many parts of the world.

The Cretan figure, on the other hand, is far more intriguing in that it shows a kind of dressing that is completely out of context with the traceable course of the history of clothes. Nothing remotely resembling it had been recorded from the ancient world until that brilliant but somewhat wayward archaeologist, Sir Arthur Evans, started his momentous excavations in Crete in the last years of the nineteenth century. There he found overwhelming evidence of a highly developed culture of 3000–1500 BC, similar to what Heinrich Schliemann had discovered at Troy and Mycenae some thirty years before. He not only shook the world of archaeology but also, incidentally, contributed something to the lesser matter of the accepted view of the history of clothes throughout the ages.

The significance of these long-lost ladies is that they show, very early and by an accident of survival and a trick of time, what was to happen aeons later in the Western World. But between them and the valid history of fashion and underwear is another chasm in time and space. The corseted figures in particular can only baffle and tease one out of thought.

When, several hundreds of years later, the era began that was to culminate in classical Greece, men and women alike were still wearing clothes formed of draped and folded lengths of material— the familiar classical draperies seen in great variety in the wealth of Greek sculpture, frescoes and vases that remain. They are shown with a detail and naturalness absent from the formalised and geometric lines of Egyptian art.

In classical Greece, as in Egypt, there were frequently two layers of clothing, worn similarly by men and women alike, but neither ranked as underwear, though they pin-pointed its origin. The chiton or tunic was knee-length or full length. It was either draped round the body and over one or both shoulders or else it was held on the shoulders by brooches or pins. Women often chose the latter effect, and both men and women sometimes added a belt to hold it in at the waist. Sometimes there were also crossed bands that went

Ionic chiton 5th century BC –2nd century AD

over the shoulders and across the chest. A famous, very clear and simple example is the statue of the charioteer at Delphi.

Over the chiton went, when needed for warmth, a himation or cloak, similar in shape to the chiton and usually wrapped round the body, over the shoulders and sometimes also over the head. It varied in size. Sometimes it was the only garment worn by men, especially older men, who wore it draped round the waist and over the left shoulder, so that part of the upper body was bare. A smaller, shorter cloak was often worn but mainly by soldiers and horsemen. It was called a chlamys.

Female statues show no trace of anything being worn under the chiton, but there is literary evidence that the Greeks, innovators in so many spheres of human progress, set a lead in the relatively small matter of women's underwear and figure control. A band of linen or kid was wound round the waist and lower torso to shape and control it. It was known as the zoné, or girdle and is referred to in the Odyssey and Iliad and also by Herodotus and others. Other Greek words were also apparently descriptive of breast bands, but exactly what this implied is not clear. The apodesmos, meaning a band, breast-band or girdle, occurs in a fragment of Aristophanes and also, some five hundred years later, in the Hellenistic writer Lucian.

A similar band, called the mastodeton, or breast band, was also worn round the bust, apparently to flatten or minimise it, and not, as in more recent history, to stress its curves. Occasionally the word mastodesmos occurs with a similar meaning. But none of the records help us to establish the extent to which such bands were worn by Greek women.

At any rate the Greeks can probably be given credit for introducing, or at least presaging, the most significant items of female underclothing, the corset and the brassière, and the ones that were, many centuries later, to have more influence than any others on fashion, when this came into existence.

Clothing in ancient Rome followed closely on the lines of that in Greece and elsewhere. In Rome too, women sometimes wore bands of material round the hips and bust—a cestus or girdle is referred to by the poet Martial and seems to have been similar to the zoné, but wider, and the strophium, or breast band, is mentioned by Cicero. A Roman mosaic in Sicily shows a female athlete wearing a bikini—briefs and bra—in the fourth century AD.

Doric chiton 5th century BC —2nd century AD

*Byzantine draped cloak,
dress and under-dress
c.6th century AD*

Medieval draped robes

There is evidence that in the days of the grandeur that was Rome clothes became more ostentatious than ever before and that women wore elaborate layers of clothing, mainly as a sign of rank and importance. Some of this may have been regarded as underwear, but it is impossible to be certain and in view of the loosely draped clothing it would not be likely to have a shape and character of its own.

From these early times onwards for many centuries one is confronted with the difficulty that underwear would not be seen. While statues, vases and frescoes show some of the richness and colourfulness, the inventive patterns, designs and embroideries that decorated clothing, and while the profusion of jewellery, beads, buckles and similar adornments worn can still be seen in surviving antiquities, of underwear there is no trace. All that can be said is that in country after country, century after century, similar draped lengths of material continued to constitute clothing. Tanagra statuettes of women of the first century AD vary scarcely at all from those of fifth century BC Greece.

When, in the fourth century AD, the capital of the Roman Empire was transferred to the site of the ancient Byzantium, which became Constantinople, the Eastern influence led to the first significant change in clothing that was to influence the Western world. For the first time trousers were worn. To start with they were, as previously in the East, regarded as mainly women's wear and unmanly. Over them went tunics of varying lengths, and at times men too wore such trousers in a knee-length style under their tunics or draped clothes. Their derivation is usually regarded as Persian and they were the precursors of all subsequent trousers and other two-legged garments worn as outerwear or underwear by both sexes. In mosaics in Byzantine churches Emperors are shown wearing knee-length tunics with long narrow sleeves, long loose cloaks and occasionally with accompanying 'barbarian' trousers.

In northern Europe the Saxons and Celts wore these trousers, and from the Bronze Age onwards loose tunics or draped lengths of material were also worn there, as over most of the world.

When, in the later Middle Ages, the recorded history of clothing in Britain began to take a coherent form by means of illuminated manuscripts which are still extant, men and women were, as all over the world, still wearing loose tunics and cloaks of the familiar pattern, and trousers of some sort were also seen, usually on men.

From all these centuries there was to emerge, as the start of underwear, the man's shirt and women's chemise, both derived from the tunic, and also what would, much later, become respectively trousers, pants and women's knickers—all originating in the early trousers. As with subsequent articles of underwear, these all started as outer garments.

The beginning of fashion and of the intricate and continually varying undergarments that were to serve the main purpose of the shape-making of which fashion mainly consists came suddenly in England and in Western Europe generally at the middle of the twelfth century. This was when, for the first time since that statue of the little Cretan lady produced its fashion enigma, women began to wear clothing fitted closely to their bodies.

The woman's long, loose tunic-style dress began about 1150 to be drawn close to the figure by means of lacing at the back, sides or front, so that it became tight-fitting and waisted. There was as yet no cutting to form the waist and no separation of bodice and skirt, but the lacing created the first closely defining waistline in modern dress history. Buttons and other fastenings did not yet exist, so lacing was the obvious way to achieve this.

Why there should have been this breakaway from the age-long tradition of loose clothing at this particular juncture it is hard to say. The reason may be that the hold of the Church was weakening and the idea of romantic love, part of the new, more secular outlook, was encouraging women to reveal their attractions. Whether this was the case or not, the emergence of the waist was the start of fashion which, for centuries to come, was to consist of continually shaping and reshaping the outward appearance of the human body, so as to make it express something of the feelings and attitudes of the individual.

'Fiend of Fashion'—twelfth century shaped, laced bodice, from Cottonian MS

It also provided the real beginning of the story of underwear. The prototype of the corset, the chief shapemaker, appears in a twelfth-century manuscript in the famous Cottonian collection, presented to the British nation by Sir John Cotton in 1700 and now in the British Museum. The collection includes medieval manuscripts and one of these shows the Devil, represented as a woman, as monastic illustrators were fond of doing. The figure, which has a human form but a grotesque, malevolent bird-like head, outspread wings and webbed feet, wears a tight-fitting bodice extending from the shoulders to below the waist and closely laced up the front, with a dangling lace falling below it almost to the ground. There is a strange tulip-shaped skirt, so long that it is knotted up in a big loop to keep it from trailing on the ground.

This is the earliest record of the shapemaker that was to become the corset, and it is momentous in underwear history for this reason. It is, however, evidently an outer garment and it was not until some three centuries later that similar items of wear were to become undergarments. This fact, however, in no way invalidates its importance as an innovation in the history of fashion and above all of underwear.

By the thirteenth century, however, women were again wearing long, loose shapeless dresses, pouched over a girdle at the waist, and with no figure definition at all. Again, it is impossible to reason or speculate why this happened.

In the mid-fourteenth century, the fitted, tightly-waisted fashion came back, this time to stay. Men as well as women began to wear clothes that were shaped to the body and from now on there was to be no looking back to the centuries of loose drapery or softly-falling shapeless robes.

Shapes would come and shapes would go, but this was the real beginning of fashion. From now on fashion was established and it was to proceed on its way, continually shaping and re-shaping the human form in ways that, in retrospect, form a panorama that is often even more bewildering and more difficult to comprehend than are those millenia when the idea of creating clothes with a shape apparently was not visualised by anyone anywhere—except perhaps those ancient Cretans.

In the process of shaping, underclothes were to play a main part and would pass through changes as many and as bewildering as would fashion itself. Without them outer fashion would not have been able to exist at all. Underwear, moreover, would have its own fashions and at many times be as sophisticated as outer fashion.

This, however, was for the future. At first the shape was the thing, and the undergarments that created it were to be primarily functional and usually carefully contrived. This in itself was, indeed, a step forward. In the Middle Ages, the religious idea had prevailed that the body was sinful and underwear therefore something rather shameful. The hair shirt was a garment of penance. People did penance and indicated their humility or shame by appearing in only their shirts or smocks (the early Saxon word for chemise) on pilgrimages or when craving the forgiveness of the Church. They therefore cannot have taken pride in their underwear.

Fashion was born as the Middle Ages ended but the centuries-old tradition of loose robes died hard. It persists to this day in ecclesiastical, legal, academic and other formalised or ceremonial clothing. It continued to be manifest for a century or two more in paintings and frescoes. Biblical and historical figures in European paintings by the great masters of the fifteenth and sixteenth centuries are continually shown wearing such robes. They are depicted with immense grandeur and often in gorgeous colourfulness in the works of such painters as Bellini, Titian, Veronese and Raphael, although some of these also show the new stiff, tight bodices that were the start of fashion.

Fashion, moreover, has remained to this day a Western monopoly. Elsewhere it has no appreciable existence except when and where the populace has been 'converted' to Western ways, thereby sharing in a wealth of new means of communication between nations. These links are particularly strong in the visual sphere.

15th century draped robes, from a painting

2 | *Towards the Elizabethans:*
1350–1600

Almost all fashion's developments have centred upon the waist and have usually been dictated by its being narrowed, lowered, raised or, for one or two brief periods, deliberately obliterated. In all the immense variety of shapes created in this way—mostly artificial and almost incredible today because they have borne little or no resemblance to the natural human shape—the waist has been the pivot on which fashion has revolved. Underwear has very largely been dominated and conditioned by this fact.

The fashionable waist has rarely been entirely natural and some way of outlining or emphasising it has been in existence from the earliest days of fashion. In some early effigies on surviving monuments and brasses, dating from the fourteenth and fifteenth centuries, there seem to be signs that something like the Greek zoné and its variations in the ancient world was worn to cinch the waist.

From the fourteenth century the moulding of the waist, previously contrived, in its brief twelfth-century emergence, by drawing together and lacing up a naturally loose robe to the shape of the body, was achieved by cutting the outer garment to the appropriately waisted pattern, as has been done ever since. People at this time were learning how to shape clothes and skill in making-up was developing as the medieval local craft guilds became more organised and efficient. The biggest development in this respect came in the reign of Queen Elizabeth, when the vigorous driving force of Cecil and the Privy Council created something like a national policy of wages, prices, apprenticeship and conditions of work in the clothing, as in other trades.

Long before that time the bodices of women's dresses had become long and narrow and the dresses, instead of being all in one piece, were joined to a flowing skirt at the hips, where a decorative belt was worn in the fourteenth century. Buttons were invented at this time and are seen on many effigies, including that of Anne of Bohemia, wife of Richard II, in Westminster Abbey. They were not, however, used in underclothes until the seventeenth century, tapes and ribbons being employed there when fastenings were necessary.

Dress of about 1150 with slim waist and girdle

Under the tight, elongated bodices there was worn, in addition to the traditional voluminous chemise, a stiffened linen underbodice. This was originally known as a 'cotte', an early French word used for any close-fitting garment and similar in meaning to *côte*, the word for ribs. As the cult of the slim figure progressed, this garment was made increasingly figure-defining and rigid by the use of paste as a stiffener between two layers of linen.

The 'cotte' thus became the earliest form of what we call the corset, and therefore one of the most important developments in the history of underwear. This stiffened bodice became known from the fifteenth century as a 'body' or 'pair of bodys', and from the seventeenth century the alternative word 'stays' came into current use. In French it was called, similarly, a 'corps' or, in an earlier spelling, 'cors'. It was at times a laced bodice, usually worn as an outer garment by women. It still survives in this form in the traditional national dress of many European countries. It has been suggested that the modern word corset was the result either of adding the diminutive 'et' to 'cors' or of linking 'serrer', meaning to close tightly, to the word 'cors'. The 'body' became more recognisably the forerunner of the corset when, in the sixteenth century, it began to be fortified with whalebone. It was the usual foundation of the increasingly rigid, elongated outer bodices that continued to characterise fashion then and in the following centuries, and it kept such bodices geometrically straight-lined. It made their severe shape possible. Sometimes the whalebone bodice was itself an outer garment, made of appropriately rich materials. Examples of this emergence of an inner as an outer garment were a recurrent feature of fashion history and some actual garments of this kind have survived from the eighteenth century and are preserved in costume collections.

Various references to the corset by name occur in surviving records from the thirteenth century onwards. It was for long taken for granted that the garment was what we call the corset, but within the past century increasing doubts and denials have been voiced on this subject by costume experts. It now appears that earlier writers on costume had confused the medieval Latin word 'corsettus' with their own term corset—a confusion which on the surface is supported by references in medieval literature to the smallness of ladies' waists.

The error was possibly started by Joseph Strutt, one of the

earliest writers on medieval life, who wrote in the late eighteenth century: 'Towards the conclusion of the fourteenth century, the women were pleased with the appearance of a long waist; and in order to produce that effect, they invented a strange disguisement called a corse or corset'. This was accepted and it took a long time to unmask his own 'strange disguisement' in the use of the word.

Many early records point to a quite different garment under the name of a corset and they all indicate an outer garment. The household accounts book of Eleanor, Countess of Leicester, for the date May 25th 1265, contains an item: 'For 9 ells, Paris measure, for summer robes, corsets and cloaks for the same . . . Richard, King of the Normans and Edward his son'. Corsets in this context seem quite out of place. In 1299 a wardrobe account of Edward I refers to a corset of miniver, which is squirrel fur and therefore even less apt. A manuscript of about 1530 describes 'her seneschal . . . mounted on a great courser, and in a rich corset of grene, girt wit a white silken lace'. Again the description is wide of the mark— a corset would not be visible.

Dr. Joan Evans, an outstanding authority on the Middle Ages, concludes after close study of the subject that the early 'corset' was 'a cloak of oval cut varying in length'. This seems to fit the available evidence. A similar view is voiced by Kay Staniland in a detailed account of the problem of the early corset. She subscribes to the view that the stays/corset developed from the stiffened 'body' or bodice of the sixteenth century, but she believes that the medieval 'corsettus' was something quite different. First applied to men's garments, in the thirteenth century, and in the fourteenth to those of women, it is usually one of several garments forming a 'robe'— tunic, supertunic, cloak or mantle and/or corsettus, all made from the same material. These materials varied from thick woollens to the richest of embroidered silks and velvets, lined with wool or more often, fur.

Drs. C. Willett and Phillis Cunnington, differentiate between the early and the later corset, but describe the earlier one as a close-fitting bodice and record that the word 'corset' began to be used as a refinement for stays at the close of the eighteenth century. Other evidence confirms this: *The Times* of 24 June 1795 said that 'corsettes about six inches long, and a slight buffon tucker of two inches high, are now the only defensive paraphernalia of our fashionable Belle'. In the following year the specifications of a patent referred to 'an improvement in the making of stays and corsettes'. From then, the term became an accepted one.

Important as this distinction about the corset is, because of its effect on much-quoted early allusions to the garment, it does not change the actual course of fashion or the story of underwear. The first dominant fashion trend was the narrow waist and the first significant article of underwear, as opposed to the timeless chemise, was the stiffened bodice. An early poem says, in obvious praise:

The lady was clad in purple pall
With gentill body and middle small.

Chaucer writes of ladies of quality in his time, the late fourteenth century, as 'clad in rich kirtle, their bodies being long and small.' The poet Gower at the same period gives a similar picture of the admired female figure:

He seeth hir shape forthwith, all
Hir body round, hir middle small.

Dunbar, the Scottish poet, in 'The Thistle and the Rose', says of some beauties that 'their middles were as small as wands'.

Under these narrow bodices with their slim waists the chemise was at first the only known item of underwear. Loose, wide, long-sleeved and ankle-length, and made of linen or cotton in its original guise, it remained so for centuries, even though the outer fashionable shape became closely defined at the waist. Chaucer in the 'Romaunt of the Rose', written about 1370, says:

. . . through her smocke ywrought with silke
The fleshe was sene as white as milke.

This makes it evident that even in early times very fine materials were sometimes used for the chemise.

Together with the narrower bodices and the 'cotte' or 'body' worn under it came an increasing width in skirts. This went on steadily from the fourteenth century through Tudor times to the fantastic extravagances of Elizabethan fashion. Under the wider skirts petticoats were worn, but exactly when this became customary is not known. Certain early manuscripts and paintings, of the late fourteenth and the fifteenth centuries, show skirts held up and evident petticoats appearing underneath them. Fastened round the waist with tapes or ribbons, these petticoats became something of a status symbol, the number worn being evidence of rank or wealth or awareness of fashion. The petticoats were of wool, linen or cotton and often coloured. There are early references to red being used,

Early fifteenth century dress

Fur-trimmed dress looped up
at side to show petticoat. c. 1450

so that the famous 'red flannel petticoat' of Victorian days has a very long pedigree. In addition to petticoats there was, however, also the kirtle. This was an underdress of which the skirt frequently was visible. Manuscripts of the period show the contemporary fashion of skirts that swept the ground to the extent of nearly a yard round the wearer's ankles. In one case the skirt is held up and under it appears a long kirtle, which is also loopĕd up to keep it from trailing.

Skirts became increasingly full during the fifteenth century. Clothes were also gradually being made of richer and richer materials. This was due mainly to the rise in trade and to the pouring into Western Europe of the rich culture of the Byzantine and post-classical world, which followed the fall of Constantinople in 1453. Among the new imports were luxury fabrics of great stiffness and richness, which were used for clothes. These obviously could not be shown to effect in the clinging, softly falling styles used for clothes made of the earlier native-born woollens.

15th century dress showing chemise at neck and cuffs

Velvet gown with open skirt, showing ornate petticoat, and split sleeves, revealing chemise c.1530–40

In order to show off the new fabrics to advantage full, bell-shaped skirts came into fashion, with, at first, numerous petticoats to enhance the shape. By the time of Henry VIII skirts were often open down the front, revealing an under-skirt or petticoat of equally splendid material underneath. This continued through the Elizabethan period, when silk, velvet, taffeta, grosgrain and satin were all used. In some cases the petticoat also seems to have been quilted or padded for extra width—and probably warmth.

The art of wearing gorgeous silks, satins, damasks, velvets and brocades to full effect was first manifest in Spain and Italy. These countries were the spearhead of the Renaissance and the fashions started there caused a revolution in dress which soon spread widely through Western Europe. The sumptuous materials were stiff and weighty. They had to stand out firmly and grandly, so the human frame became a kind of mobile scaffolding to support the splendour which the Elizabethans loved in dress, as in other aspects of their exuberant life.

The chief device used to achieve this effect transformed skirts. The full bell-shaped Tudor ones, held out by petticoats and kirtle, were not enough for the Elizabethans, whose lives were an extravaganza of creative energy and vitality poured into whatever they did, whether it was exploration, literature, drama, art or zestful, rumbustious living. Fashion, both for men and women, went to wild extremes and decreed that both sexes should look twice as large as nature made them.

By the 1550's, in the reign of Mary Tudor, who had married Philip II of Spain in 1554, skirts began to be made enormous by being artificially supported from underneath by the farthingale, of which two types were introduced. First came the Spanish farthingale. It probably started as a petticoat 'boosted' by a series of graduated corded hoops, but soon the hoops were of cane, whalebone or wire. In its more modest manifestations the farthingale was almost a perfect replica of the Cretan lady's skirt of 3500 years before, but it grew wider and wider, until, by the late 1550's, it was a separate framework over which the petticoats and skirt were draped. The source, Spain, was a 'natural' one as Spain at this time was the most powerful country in Western Europe, with dominion from 1579 not only over its own native territory but also over Germany, the Netherlands, parts of Italy and the new world across the Atlantic.

Spanish farthingale, mid 16th century

Mid 16th century dress showing Spanish farthingale

French farthingale c.1580

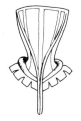

'Body' with steel bands and busk and long tapering point in front c.1580

Dress worn over French farthingale c.1580

Dress with French farthingale and ruff c.1600

The farthingale was originally a Court fashion, contrived to display in full the splendour of the fabrics which were by then being used for clothes, but it spread to some extent elsewhere, although its vogue does not seem to have been so general as that of the eighteenth-century hoops and the nineteenth-century crinoline. In Elizabethan times the barrier between Court circles and the fashionable world on the one hand and the rest of the populace on the other was greater than in subsequent periods, and the peasant population, living on the land, was larger. One obviously could not work there in the panoply of a farthingale.

The sizes of the farthingale became immense, as is recorded in Heywood's *Epigrams,* published in 1590:

Alas, poor verdingales must lie in the streete,
To house them no doore in the citee made meete,
Syns at our narrow doores they on can not win,
Send them to Oxforde, at Brodegates to get in.

During the late 1570's a different type of farthingale, known as the French one, was introduced, and was even more grotesque. It consisted of a kind of vast horizontal hoop worn at the waist, but tilted down at the front to accommodate the elongated front of the stiffened bodice. Over it, again, were draped the petticoats and

skirts, the latter usually of fantastically rich materials, and sometimes open down the front to reveal a rich petticoat. This is the
farthingale seen in many portraits of Queen Elizabeth and in other
portraits of the time. It is the most unnatural and probably the most
uncomfortable and inconvenient garment in the whole story of
fashion. One recent writer echoes most people's opinion in describing it as 'one of the most hideous distortions that has ever
obsessed the imagination and distorted the lines of the human
body'. But in spite of a progressive waning of their popularity and a
diminishing of their size, the two styles of farthingale did not
wholly disappear until about 1625.

For those Elizabethans who did not run to such extremes of
fashion as these presented, there was an alternative—a roll or
'sausage' of stiffened material worn round the waist under the
skirts, so as to hold them out to a lesser degree. It was known as a
'bum-roll' and was to recur in later fashion.

In the late sixteenth century, stiffened bodices of an increasingly
formidable kind were also being worn, usually under the dress,
sometimes as part of it. They were, however, still always known as
a 'body' or 'pair of bodys'. Ben Jonson seems to refer to this garment
when he writes, about 1600, of

*Early 17th century hip
bolster or 'bum roll'*

'*The whalebone man*

That quilts the bodies I have leave to span.'

The stiffened linen bodice, with whalebone or steel to give it
rigidity, was also sometimes padded with wool. Next it was given
a front 'busc' or busk.

The busk, credited with having had its origin in Italy and with
having been brought to England by Catherine of Aragon, was the
first artificial support given to the figure. It was therefore the origin
of all the boning and other devices that were to be the basis of
corsets for the next four hundred years and which even today
have not wholly lost their importance.

The busk was originally made of wood, horn, ivory, metal or
whalebone and was at times carved or painted. It was shaped rather
like a long paper knife, thicker at the top than at the bottom, and
could extend from above the bust to the waist or even nearly to the
hips. It was slotted into the Elizabethan bodice or was part of the
'body', or early corset, and it was held in place with a lace, so that
it could be pulled in or out. It is credited with having been produced
on occasion to administer a sharp rap to an importunate male, just as

Iron corset, hinged at one side c.1530

the eighteenth century fan was. The lace, like the nineteenth-century garter, was bestowed as a special favour on the man who had found favour with the lady to whom it belonged.

The busk remained a feature of dress in many succeeding periods and it has continued to be an important component of 'stays' and corsets right up to the present century. It still exists in a few of the remaining very traditional corset designs.

By the second half of the sixteenth century whalebone was also being used at the sides and back of the 'body' which was laced up the front. A stomacher, a stiffened strip of material reaching from bust to below waist, was worn behind the front lacing under the open-fronted dresses of the second half of the sixteenth century. As the Elizabethan fashion for very stiff, elongated bodices developed, with the front of the bodice extending to a point as low as was compatible with being able to sit down, the 'body' became even more severe, to give the required fashionable, almost tube-like straightness to the bodice of the dress. It was sometimes made of leather and whalebone, and as it encased the body from above the bust almost to the hips it must have been an instrument of near-torture.

Catherine de Medici, wife of Henry II of France (1579–1589), who was something of a fashion dictator in her time, is believed to have frowned on a thick waist as amounting to the height of bad manners and to have prescribed thirteen inches as the ideal. She is also said to have introduced a particularly rigid and powerful 'corps', hardened and stiffened and rising almost to the throat, so that the effect was to create almost a drainpipe shape.

Tradition has it that she was also the originator of the much-discussed iron corset of the time. This looked almost like a piece of armour, made in an openwork design over which silk or velvet could be stretched. It was hinged at one side and closed at the other with a hasp or pin. A few examples still exist. Some students of fashion believe it was worn as an outer garment, in addition to the accepted stiff 'body', but there is now also a more widely held view that it was a remedial or surgical type of garment and not one intended for ordinary wear.

The stiffened 'body' as it actually existed was, however, formidable enough. It was satirically and scornfully described by Philip Gosson in 1591 in his 'Pleasant Quippes for Upstart Newfangled Gentlewomen':

These privie coates by art made strong,
With bones, with paste and suchlike ware,
Whereby their backe and sides grew long
And now they harnest gallants are;
Were they for use against the foe,
Our dames for Amazons might goe.

But seeing they doe only stay
The course that nature doth intend,
And mothers often by them slay
Their daughters yoong, and worke their end;
What are they els but armours stout,
Wherein like gyants Jove they flout?

Although, unlike the 'body' and the farthingale, it cannot be classified as an undergarment, the ruff, that other dominating feature of the Elizabethan lady's apparel, derives directly from underwear. Its origin lay in the edging of the chemise, which was often visible at the neckline of dresses. Such an edging was frequently embroidered either in white or in black and examples of Elizabethan 'black embroidery' still exist, including one in the Victoria and Albert Museum. When lace was invented in the sixteenth century it was used and seen at the neck of chemises, and from this the ruff started about 1550 as a quite separate item of dress. To begin with it was small, but its dimensions increased gradually. Its vogue, for both men and women, was closely bound up with the introduction into England of starch. This was effected in 1564 by a Dutch woman, a Madame Dingham van der Plasse, and it made it possible to wear a deep ruff which would stand up by itself. In the grandoise Elizabethan manner the ruff could rise as high as the top of the wearer's head at the back. Stubbs writes scornfully: 'There is a certain liquid matter which they call starch, wherein the devil hath learned them to wash and dive their ruffs, which, being dry, will then stand stiff and inflexible about their necks'. Some ruffs were so vast that spoons were made with specially long handles to enable the wearers to eat. Unlike the farthingale the ruff continued to be worn during a great part of the seventeenth century. It is seen in several portraits by Rembrandt, including two of Margaretta Tripp, one of which is dated 1663, and one of an eighty-three year old woman. Van Dyck (1599–1641) also testifies to the continued wearing of the ruff by showing it in his portraits.

Fashionable starched ruff
c.1585

Stockings are not usually included in underwear, although for centuries they were almost concealed, in the case of women at any rate, and therefore could claim to be 'underneaths.' Today we classify them rather as accessories, but their close connection with underwear and especially with knitting associated with underwear earns a mention of how and when they came into the clothing picture.

While weaving is one of the earliest of human activities, knitting is rather different. It cannot claim a continuous history, but it probably started in Arabia in the second century AD. It was known in Europe in the Middle Ages, and was important enough to have its own Guild, with men and women both engaged in it. It was not, however until Elizabethan times that knitted stockings came to be generally worn. Leg coverings up to then had usually been made of cloth, like gaiters. The first knitted stockings, hand-made of course, were silk ones imported from Spain at a luxury price. They were, however, followed by cheaper worsted ones. The trade grew rapidly and spread widely over England, mainly in the areas already concerned with wool.

Nottingham, as a great wool town, became an early centre of the hand-knitting industry. Near there, in Calverton, in 1589, William Lee, a poor parson, invented a machine for knitting stockings more quickly than by hand. After demonstrating his machine, with the aim of securing a patent for it, he presented Queen Elizabeth with a pair of silk stockings made on it. While she admired them, she was afraid of an invention which to her seemed likely to put people in the hand-knitting trade out of work. Disappointed over his failure to obtain a patent, Lee took his invention to France. After his death in 1610 his brother brought back a few of his machines to London and Nottingham and the frame-knitting trade was established in this way.

London and the South, being near to the Spitalfields silk market and situated at the hub of fashion, concentrated on the manufacture of silk stockings. In Nottingham trade, growing more slowly, was built up on the substantial worsted stockings produced from the long-fibred wool of Sherwood sheep. This trade spread throughout the seventeenth century. Hand-knitted and frame-knitted hosiery co-existed without the disruption Queen Elizabeth had feared, and hand-knitted goods were still a considerable export in the latter part of the eighteenth century.

The rather gradual development of the trade was due to the slowness of the process of yarn-spinning. It took eight spinners to keep one weaver at work. The speeding up of yarn production was the result of Hargreaves' invention, in 1764, of the spinning jenny, which meant that several spindles could operate on one spinning wheel, and of Arkwright's 1767 improvement on this. His great contribution was a machine which spun yarn by the roller method. Like a host of subsequent mechanical inventions in industry, both these achievements caused widespread labour troubles based on the recurrent fear of human labour being superseded. But they proved to be landmarks in the progress of textiles and clothing. The immense part taken by knitting machines in all the variety of underwear which was to be worn by the whole community in the nineteenth and twentieth centuries had its origin in that sixteenth-century stocking machine of William Lee.

3 | *Hoops and Stays: 1600–1790*

The Elizabethan style of dress lingered on until about 1625, when Charles I's Queen, French-born Henrietta Maria, introduced a new and different trend—softer, more flowing and gracious—which was largely French in origin.

Instead of the rigidly built-up figure, there was a far less formal look. The stiff, ostentatious brocades and jewelled and heavily embroidered materials gave way to lighter silks, many of them from Lyons, where the silk industry was expanding rapidly. Colours, hitherto strong and violently contrasted, also became softer.

The seventeenth century, with its chequered political history, presented a number of fashion swings in a comparatively short time for these days, but the dominating change was to more natural skirts, still held out by petticoats but not artificially supported. The top petticoat, or underskirt, was frequently visible to a large extent throughout seventeenth-century fashions. This was done in two ways. Skirts were very long, and even had trains, but were often slit up the front to show the underskirt. The skirt was also very often, except on special occasions, worn looped up or tucked into the waist, probably to prevent it from trailing on the ground and getting soiled. The petticoat therefore became of paramount importance.

As seventeenth-century fashions began to evolve, the waistline started by becoming higher and, with the disappearance of the ruff, the edge of the chemise, probably lace-trimmed or embroidered, was also frequently seen at the neckline. Sleeves, which were sometimes three-quarter length instead of coming down to the wrist, as in the previous period, were often slashed or partly formed of vertical bands of ribbon, so that the sleeves of the chemise were visible through and below them.

The actual body remained firmly controlled under 'bodys' which during the seventeenth century started to become known as stays. These stays came high up on the torso and were stiffened by the usual whalebone. There was also continued emphasis on a slim waist and, as the seventeenth century progressed, there was an

Slit skirt, looped up to show petticoat. Low neck and short sleeves, showing chemise underneath c.1670

Silk gown pinned up at sides to show taffeta petticoat c.1630

Dress with split sleeves showing full sleeves of chemise c.1650

increase in the tight lacing which was to persist for nearly two centuries, with only one or two brief remissions. This led to the epithets 'strait-laced' and 'staid' under the Puritan régime of the mid-century which, instead of condemning this extremity of fashion, commended tight-lacing on the grounds that it disciplined the body—a theory quite contrary to the original purpose of allurement.

During the eleven years of the Commonwealth clothes became plain and severe, at any rate among the Roundheads, and, although the temporarily eclipsed Cavaliers presumably did not conform closely to this, the effect was to discourage decorative and rich dressing.

All that changed, however, when Charles II came to the throne, full of ideas from France, where he and his family and supporters had been in exile. Silks, velvets, an abundance of lace, ribbons (tied in a confusion of innumerable bows all over the clothes of both men and women) and feathers all abounded. But the general effect was much looser and easier than for a long time. Though bodices remained stiff and sometimes boned, the provocative effect of the slightly casual and nonchalant look was exploited.

Cotton chemise with finely pleated sleeves and low front c.1750

Pepys' diary reflects the interest taken in clothes after the Restoration, although it is noticeable that, like many men of his time, he is far more concerned with his own finery than with his wife's. There are, however, frequent references to what she wore. On 18th August 1660 he says: 'Towards Westminster by water. I landed my wife at Whitefriars with £5 to buy her a petticoat, and my father persuaded her to buy a most fine cloth, of 26s. a yard, and a rich lace, so that the petticoat will come to £5; but she doing it very innocently, I could not be angry.' Next day he writes: 'Home to dinner, where my wife had on her new petticoat that she bought yesterday, which indeed is a very fine cloth and a fine lace, but that being of a light colour, and the lace all silver, it makes no great show.' This makes it clear that the petticoat was visible to a conspicuous extent and could make a 'great show'.

The chemise, stays and petticoats still remained the only underwear worn. Although drawers had become part of feminine apparel in some continental countries, notably Italy, they were not worn in this country until the early nineteenth century, from about 1815, when, very oddly, they were at first looked on as being bold and immodest—because they were adopted by women after being an exclusively male garment in the past few centuries.

Few as undergarments were, they showed one significant development in the seventeenth century. They had sex-appeal. The lace or embroidered edging of the chemise at neck and sleeves, its low neck and finely pleated sleeves, the visible outer petticoat and glimpses of other petticoats, revealed by softer outer clothes, all contributed to this deliberate effect, which was wholly absent from the cage-like or drum-shaped Elizabethan clothes, whose purpose would seem mainly to have been self-aggrandisement, for both men and women. There was sex-appeal too in the increasingly casual look of women's dress. The feeling is voiced by the Cavalier poets, notably by Herrick, who wrote his poem 'The Poetry of Dress' about 1650:

> *A sweet disorder in the dress*
> *Kindles in clothes a wantonness:*
> *A lawn about the shoulders thrown*
> *Into a fine distraction,*
> *An erring lace which here and there*
> *Enthrals the crimson stomacher*
> *A cuff neglectful, and thereby*

Ribands to flow confusedly,
A winning wave, deserving note,
In the tempestuous petticoat,
A careless shoe-string, in whose tie
I see a wild civility,
Do more bewitch me than when art
Is too precise in every part.

It is from this time that actual evidence of what clothes were like begins to build up. The Costume Museum at Bath has early seventeenth-century women's waistcoats and other accessories and also a probably unique complete and very beautiful Restoration dress. Sir Peter Lely's portraits show contemporary seventeenth-century clothes in detail and with a feeling for the effect they produced. The London Museum has a bodice of blue moiré silk of 1650–60 and the Victoria and Albert Museum another of about 1660 in white satin. Both these are boned—a fashion which, would provide a substitute for stays. This was, however, short-lived and by about 1670 the boned bodice had again been displaced by separate stays as a means of shaping the body from underarms to waist.

From about 1670 the stays became longer, going below the waist at front and back with tabbed side-pieces below the waist stiffened with whalebone to shape the figure there, indenting it at the waist and adding curves at the hips. They were laced back or front and had an increasing amount of whalebone inserted into them and stitched closely in place—always, of course, by hand.

From now on surviving bodices, stays, petticoats and various kinds of hoops and panniers provide ample evidence of the extent to which whalebone, already established as the favourite shape-maker, continued to contribute to the stays, petticoats and artificial devices that gave the feminine figure the contours of fashion and built it up into all the eccentricities that elegance prescribed.

Why, it might well be asked, whalebone? There must be good reasons why whalebone should have remained for centuries the chief material used for shaping stays and corsets and giving them the firmness and figure-controlling qualities which were the main function of the garments. So general was its use that to this day 'bones' are the normal description of corset stiffeners, though almost always the 'bones' now consist of piral steel or plastic. There are even such contradictory descriptions as 'spiral steel bones' and 'plastic bones'.

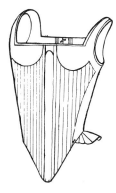

17th century stays

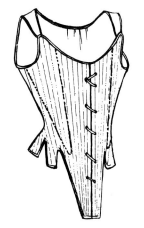

Early 18th century stays

The story of whalebone in corsetry is told by Norah Waugh in her *Corsets and Crinolines*. One main reason for its choice was that it had an elasticity, springiness and flexibility that were unequalled by anything else until spiral steels and elastic began to be used, well on in the nineteenth century. It also kept the shape given to it by heating and cooling under compression, which was particularly important in the elaborately waisted eighteenth- and nineteenth-century corset. It could, in addition, be split as finely as could be desired for close boning, without losing its efficiency.

Whalebone originally came from the Bay of Biscay, where there was a whaling industry as early as the twelfth century. In the later Middle Ages whalebones were used as stiffening for headdresses, plumes and the long, fantastically pointed shoes worn by fashionable men in the fifteenth century. By the seventeenth century whales were almost extinct in the Bay of Biscay, but the industry moved to Greenland, where the Dutch were the main operators of it. This lasted until nearly the end of the eighteenth century, during which the vogue for hooped skirts, as well as stiff stays, caused whalebone to be in great demand. By the nineteenth century the Arctic Ocean was replacing the exhausted Greenland whaling grounds, and in the period when the crinoline was in fashion, from about 1850 to 1870, the demand for whalebone was greater than ever before and the shortage of supplies at times became acute. It was opportune that, during the nineteenth century, steel began to replace it, even though steel did not become a really satisfactory corset stiffener until stainless steel began to be used commercially on a large scale after Brearly's discovery in Sheffield in 1912 that it was an ideal material for cutlery. The story of steel in corsetry belongs mainly to the twentieth century, but the use of whalebone still falls within the living memory of some people.

A further step towards a return to artificial shaping as a feature of fashion began towards the end of the seventeenth century. The looping and bunching up of skirts towards the back had during the century been putting emphasis on that part of the figure, and it was logical that this should lead to the wearing of a bustle. This was sometimes, as in Elizabethan days, called a 'bum roll' and consisted of a pad made of cork or stuffed with some kind of cushion filling. It was tied to the waist and boosted out the figure at the back.

How elaborate was the dress of the early eighteenth century is evidenced by a description in *The Manners and Customs of London in the Eighteenth Century,* which says: 'The ladies must have exhibited a wonderful appearance in 1709; behold one equipped with a black silk petticoat, with a red and white calico border, cherry coloured stays trimmed with blue and silver, a red and dove coloured damask gown flowered with large trees; a yellow satin apron trimmed with white Persian (silk), and muslin head clothes with crow-foot edging, double ruffles with fine edging, a black silk furbelowed scarf, and a spotted hood'.

The trend of fashion to hoops and panniers, which resembled to some extent the Elizabethan farthingales, is also described in 1711 in the words of Sir Roger de Coverley who, while referring to his family pictures, says: 'You see, Sir, my great-great grandmother has on the new-fashioned petticoat except that the modern is gathered at the waist; my grandmother appeared as if she stood in a large drum, whereas the ladies now walk as if they were in a go-cart'.

The chief importance of the revived bustle was that it was the precursor of the hooped petticoat which came into fashion from about 1710 and was to dominate women's dress for most of that century. This contrivance, reminiscent of the farthingale, passed through various forms, but the general effect was to widen the figure to an extravagant degree at the sides. To start with, however, it was bell-shaped and consisted of three or more hoops of wood, metal or cane, suspended on tapes from the waist. This was the form it took until about 1740. Then it was flattened at back and front and sometimes became a pair of panniers extending at each side. These were sometimes part of the petticoat, the hoops being stitched on to the material of that garment. Sometimes the panniers were a separate contraption, covered with material and attached by tapes at each

Stays, chemise, petticoat and panniers, mid 18th century

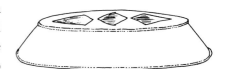

Side hoops, c.1750, of cane, covered with green flowered silk

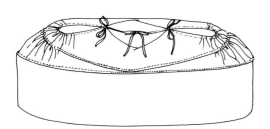

Pink Holland hoops stiffened with cane or whalebone c.1770

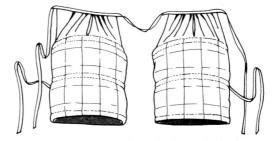

Panniers in pink and white checked linen, stiffened with cane c. 1730–50

side of the waist. Soon cane was replaced by whalebone, which was more pliable and more easily manoeuvred for some such heady adventure as getting through doors sideways when wearing hoops.

The fashion was repeatedly attacked by caricaturists, who declared that women looked like donkeys carrying baskets. In 1753 there appeared a pamphlet called 'The Enormous Abomination of the Hoop Petticoat as the Fashion now is.' The amount of space taken up by the hoop was often a social problem. The announcement of the first performance of Handel's 'Messiah' in *Faulkner's Journal,* Dublin, April 13, 1742, says: 'The Stewards of the Charitable Musical Society request the favour of the ladies not to come with hoops this day to the Musick Hall in Fishamble Street. The Gentlemen are desired to come without their swords.'

Clothes were much lighter than in Elizabethan times and as the eighteenth century progressed there was an increasing vogue for dresses of soft, hand-painted silks and for muslins and lawns, giving the floating, negligent look seen in Watteau's paintings. The hooped skirt was not the solid, immovable framework that the farthingale had been. On the contrary, it was always liable to be blown about (and even turned inside out) by the wind or sudden movement or an

Taffeta dress with full panniers, skirt looped back with bows to show flower-sprigged silk petticoat c.1725

Cotton chemise, trimmed with lace c.1747

unwary step. The provocative effect of the exposed ankle or leg was made much of and the plight of the lady whose hooped skirt was swept upwards was the theme of gaily ribald jests among the men of the time. It was also the fashion to give the hooped skirt a slight tilt when walking, so that the under-petticoats became provocatively visible. White stockings, then just coming into fashion, enhanced this effect. In the pseudo-simplicity and elaborate naiveté of the time it was also a favourite diversion of young men to send their young ladies flying gaily through the air on swings. Before this exploit was undertaken the perilous hooped skirt was tied tightly round the wearer's ankles, usually with the man's hat-band, but the possibility of an accident was an intriguing accompaniment of this sport.

By the mid-eighteenth century hoops reached fantastic dimensions. Henry Fielding, the novelist, refers to 'seven yards of hoop' and another writer to eight yards. Reproofs about the shortness of the petticoats underneath are also voiced. The petticoats were often no more than calf length, of light material and very slim. The only other article of underwear worn, apart from the stays, was the chemise, still usually knee-length or longer, so that the raising of the hooped skirt in walking would be very revealing, in terms of what was usually seen of feminine limbs in these days.

About 1760 a new kind of hoop was invented. It consisted of hinged iron hoops worn at each side of the waist. These could be lifted to enable the wearer to pass through narrow spaces. Over this contraption the outer skirt was fitted with immense care, so that among the fashionable scarcely a crease was visible in it.

Unlike the farthingale, which had been more or less limited to Court circles and the wealthy and leisured, the hooped petticoat was commonly worn. In its extreme form it did not, however, persist for very long and by about 1780 hoops were going out. After this, false 'rumps' or 'bums' were again being worn, with skirts tucked up or looped back in many folds over full and elaborate petticoats, often quilted in intricate designs or heavily embroidered.

The bodices of dresses worn with these adventurous skirts were, by contrast, tight and rigid. They were usually long-waisted, coming down to a point in front, and under them stiff, heavily boned stays were worn throughout this century. Fashionable men were addicted to these as well as women, and girls also wore them continually from a very early age. Examples of these stays still exist

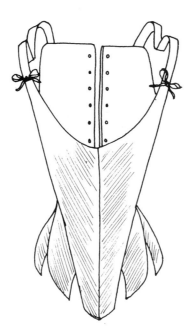

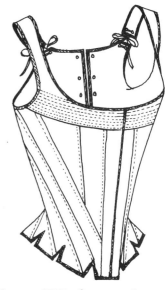

Mid 18th century stays

Stays c.1775 of maroon figured silk, edged with cream, boned and stitched

Stays, chemise and petticoat c.1780

and can be examined in costume collections at many museums. Generally speaking, they are made of rather coarse linen or cotton, closely stitched from top to bottom and with row upon row of cane or whalebone inserted in them. Sometimes these stiffeners are so narrow and so near to each other that there is scarcely room for the stitching that separates one from the other. Lacing was usually up the back, with a busk in front, but stays meant for women with heavy figures sometimes had two or three lots of lacing. The fronts of these stays were usually high, the backs even higher, and there were shoulder straps that went either on or off the shoulders, according to the style of dress being worn. Fashionable stays were often brightly coloured and made of very rich materials. One in the collection of historical clothes at Snowshill Manor is in blue damask, others in red silk and green linen.

Sometimes stays were covered with silk or brocade and sometimes with the material of the dress, so that they became the dress bodice. At other times they were embroidered, as were many of those of the following century. They were also at times built into the dress, especially if the latter was a very formal one.

How the corset could be worn as an outer bodice is indicated by an elaborate example dated about 1700, which is in the Victoria and Albert Museum. Made of rose pink watered silk, it is completely boned, as would be expected. The innumerable rows of narrow bones are stitched in so closely as to produce almost the effect of a ribbed material and the garment is completely rigid with them. There is front lacing and the shoulder straps, usual in corsetry until the early nineteenth century, are tied with ribbons at the front. There are two additions to this corset. The first is a long stomacher — a busk-like strip of stiffened material attached under the front lacing. The second is a pair of long, narrow sleeves which are tied on to the straps with ribbons. There is embroidery round the bust and the bottom of the corset, from the waist, is slashed up a few inches at spaces of two or three inches apart, so that it juts out below the waist. What the sleeves meant is uncertain; it is possible that some kind of sleeveless waistcoat, tunic or overbodice was worn over the corset.

A new note of prettiness characterises some other surviving corsets of the late eighteenth century. One, of cream silk, dated about 1780, has front and back lacing, and though it still has straps and points below the waist, it is much softer. Particularly attractive, and of the same decade, is a very different kind of corset. It is made of green glazed cotton with pink silk ribbon edging and pink and white silk embroidered motifs on the boning, which appears only in the front and under the arms. It is, of course, short below the waist, with the usual points, and there are shoulder straps above the straight front which, as usual, pushed up the bust and did not contain it.

Many stays were home-made and instructions for making them began to be published in the ladies' magazines which came into existence at the end of the seventeenth century. These publications became a fruitful source of information on fashion as by the latter part of the eighteenth century many of them carried a fashion article in each issue. At first they were wary of mentioning the 'unmentionable' underclothes, but gradually did so, and in due course, from about the eighteen-seventies, underwear advertisements also were included, thus adding to our knowledge of the subject. The fashionable woman's stay-maker was, however, an important personage in the eighteenth century. Usually he was a man, the most famous in London being Cosins. Many engravings and drawings exist showing ladies of fashion being fitted with their stays, a ritual as complicated as that required for a dress or other outerwear. In a poem of this period called the 'Bassit Table' and

Quilted petticoat c.1750–80

'False bosom', from a 1791 etching

attributed to Lady Mary Wortley Montagu, a description is given of a young newcomer to town in the words of Similinda, an older woman who has befriended her but feels her efforts slighted:

> *She owes to me the very chains she wears—*
> *An awkward thing when first she came to town,*
> *Her shape unfashioned and her face unknown;*
> *I introduced her to the Park and plays,*
> *And by my interest Cosins made her stays.*

Among eighteenth-century underwear there was also a widespread vogue for quilted petticoats, worn both for warmth and effect. One that survives, belonging to about 1730–40, is in blue satin quilted in a lozenge-shaped design, interlined with cotton-wool and lamb's wool and backed with grey woollen cloth. Others, also still in existence, are in white and pink silk and pale blue and fawn satin, quilted with cotton wool in elaborate patterns, especially at the hem. Often they are quilted onto a glazed woollen cloth which was known as callamanca.

This elaborate quilting reached its zenith during the latter part of the century but it started about 1740, when skirts were often open in front and looped back to display the quilting. The petticoat was therefore an important part of the dress, but was still called a petticoat. Simple quilting continued for many years for ordinary people. Petticoats during this century were also edged with flounces and frills, and in some cases were made of the same material as the dress. Towards the end of the century another artifice was adopted —a pad that boosted out the bosom, so that the lady projected both before and aft. This was much caricatured at the time, special spoons being suggested in order to make eating a possibility, just as they had been in the days of the ruff.

4 | *Change, then the Crinoline: 1790−1870*

Towards the end of the eighteenth century fashion's changes seemed to be proceeding within a fairly predictable pattern, successive artificial widening of the figure being followed by less exaggerated styles, but both supported by all-important petticoats. The farthingale and hoops had already demonstrated this cycle, and the crinoline was to repeat it in the nineteenth century. In each of the two earlier cases chemises and petticoats had persisted. The tyranny of the small waist had also been accepted without much demur, presumably on the principle of *'il faut souffrir pour être belle'*.

Then from France in the 1790's, coincident with the Revolution, came a fashion upheaval without precedent. It was introduced by a Paris social set known as 'Les Merveilleuses' and led by Mme Récamier and Mme Tallien and it was brought to England by the famous dressmaker, Rose Bertin, described by Madge Garland as 'that eighteenth-century amalgam of Antoine, Chanel and Elizabeth Arden,' when she fled to London during the French Revolution. Petticoats, corsets, even chemises were discarded. So were high heels, elaborate headdresses and hair styles and indeed almost all the sophisticated accessories that fashionable women had been acquiring for some two hundred years. Instead the vogue was for slim, high-waisted muslin or printed cotton shifts, clinging to the figure and worn with the minimum of underclothing and little flat shoes. Hair was cut short. Some descriptions refer to near nudity underneath them, and at times flesh-coloured tights could be the only underwear. The *Ladies' Monthly Museum* of June 1802 describes 'the close, all white, shroud looking, ghostly chemise undress of the ladies, who seem to glide like spectres, with their shrouds wrapt tight about their forms'. The same periodical in March 1803 refers to 'young ladies who were dressed or rather undressed in all the nakedness of the mode'.

Though extreme devotees of this new fashion abandoned their stays, they did sometimes condescend to wear bands wrapped round the body like the Greek zoné. There was also a tiny six-inch-deep corset as a compromise and a three-inch belt that rose to a point between the breasts. At times these muslins were damped down to make them cling more closely and revealingly to the figure. Basically the style aimed at a return to the classical Greek tunic, worn without any supporting or concealing underwear. The imitation was deliberate in that the devotees of the new French Republic were harking back to the first famous Republic—that of ancient Greece, which they regarded as the birthplace of the freedom that Revolutionary France was proclaiming. There was also an obvious link-up with the current trend of thought, typified by Rousseau's writings with their exhortation to freedom: 'Man was born free, but everywhere he is in chains'. This was the first time in the history of fashion that there had been any such 'revival' of a by-gone mode. It was also the first time that a fashion had been introduced which was specially attuned to the young.

This way of dressing spread to England, but usually it was worn on a modified scale. The thin muslin would have some underwear to accompany it, and a slim cotton lining to the dress was introduced, with a bodice formed of criss-cross bands which supported the bosom somewhat as the brassière was to do about a century and a quarter later. Short corsets were sometimes worn. There were also various styles of knee-length overdresses which accompanied the muslin shifts, presumably for warmth as well as modesty.

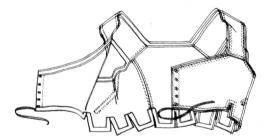

Short linen stays in blue silk, front-buttoning c.1790

Full length fine cotton chemise with buttoned tab front c.1800

It is evident from surviving examples of undergarments of the late eighteenth and early nineteenth centuries and from ladies' magazines of the time that by no means all women took to the new fashions. Records exist of the continued wearing of voluminous knee-length chemises with the usual short sleeves, though allusions are made to the fact that this garment was not always worn. Petticoats often had attached bodices, but they also were sometimes discarded by the ultra-fashionable, who wanted to look slim. Short separate bodices were also worn.

Rather oddly, drawers (as they were at first called) first became an accepted item of underwear in Britain at this time, early in the nineteenth century. As a trousered garment was regarded as an appropriation of a hitherto exclusively male item of dress, drawers were frowned upon by the conventional and were regarded as immodest instead of, as we would consider, a long-overdue concession to decorum. In 1800 a book by a Dr. Willicks said: 'In High life many women and girls wear Drawers, an abominable invention which produce disorders in abundance'.

Another new item of underwear was pantaloons, soon called pantalettes, as this was considered a more feminine and refined description. This version of the new drawers reached to below the calf, and usually had deep lace edging. Unlike drawers, pantaloons were meant to be glimpsed or seen below the skirt, but this offended the spirit of prudery which was rising in England. Probably for this reason, unlike the more reticent drawers, they had a short lifetime. There is at least one shocked reference in a contemporary diary to their being seen below the muslin transparency of the new-style dresses, but they disappeared in the 1820's except for very young girls.

Corsets, worn under clinging dresses by the not-so-slim and not-so-young, also became longer from about 1800 till 1811. They went down to the hips, instead of ending, as previously, just below the waist at a point or with tabs. They also went up high enough to push up the bust. Well-stiffened with whalebone, they now began to have rounded cup-shaped bust sections inserted in them instead of imposing on the bosom the flatness or the pushed-up look that had previously prevailed. There were other gussets below the waist to give curves to the hips. In 1816 a further extension of this trend appeared in the shape of the oddly named Divorce Corset, which did not refer to marital disagreement but to the separation of one breast

Cotton open drawers, tucked and trimmed with lace. 1825–1830

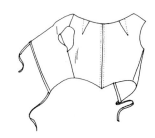

Cotton bodice, tied at back c. 1830

Long stays with removable busk, worn with drawers, early 19th century

from the other. It was achieved by means of a padded triangle of iron or steel which was inserted into the centre front of the corset with the point upwards. The principle was similar to that carried out less drastically by the modern brassière, but it was a short-lived innovation that left no mark on the solid Victorian bust line. Metal eyelets for lacings were first patented by Rogers of London in 1823, but the modern style of eyelet was devised by Daude of Paris and came into use in 1828. Steel busks were used in 1829. In 1832 Jean Werley, a Frenchman, made a landmark in corset history when he took out a patent for woven corsets made on a loom. These were popular until about 1890 and were important as the first step towards the machine-made corset.

By about 1820 the fashion for diaphanous, clinging muslins and 'Grecian' simplicity had passed and there was a recurrence of the already twice-repeated cycle of progressively widening skirts. Until about mid-century these were supported by an increasing number of petticoats, which sometimes amounted to as many as six or seven. Petticoats also became progressively wider. The underneath ones were of flannel, and over them were cotton ones, the top one probably being either embroidered, lace-trimmed or flounced. In a reaction from the provocative and colourful underwear of the eighteenth century, the early nineteenth century reverted to a chaste and decorous white, and the era of Victorian prudery began to be expressed in clothing.

The chemise was also worn, and retained its previous style, being still bulky, with sleeves, and extending to about knee-length. The wearing of drawers now became general among the upper and middle classes. Like the wearing of numerous petticoats, this had a *cachet* about it and was a kind of status symbol.

The bustle also came back soon after 1820, at first as a small, down-stuffed pad at the back, but before 1840 as a larger and more extensive addition to the natural figure, reaching round to the sides. As the middle of the nineteenth century approached skirts became increasingly full and beneath their ordinary petticoats women began to wear an additional short one of a material composed of horsehair and thread and called crinoline, from the French word *crin*, horse-hair and *linum*, thread. This was used as stiffening under hems and in sleeves. Imitations were introduced, made of stiffened silk, linen or cotton, and were also described as crinolines at least as early as 1829. From 1850, as skirts continued to become wider,

Laced-up stays, with long chemise c.1830

Corset c.1831

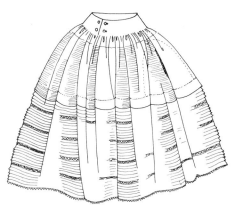

Young girl's petticoat with attached top, in white corded cotton c.1830

Petticoat in white corded cotton with tucks 1830–50

Linen chemise c.1835

crinoline fabric was used in a series of very full petticoats which boosted out the skirt. This remained fashionable until the mid 1850's.

Skirts still continued to increase in width after this, and spread out like three-dimensional fans. At this point, however, there came what seemed in some ways a liberation. To replace the insupportable bulk and weight of petticoats there was produced a framework of whalebone, wire or watch-spring steel, which could extend skirts even more—and at the same time dispense with most of the petticoats. This structure, suspended on strips of cloth and attached at the waist, was sometimes completely covered with material. Sometimes it was just a cage-like framework. Its lightness was bliss, after the heavy petticoats, and the skirt over it swung intriguingly in movement, revealing enticing glimpses of pretty ankles and feet.

The word crinoline was now used to describe the actual full skirt and Lady Longford records that the Empress Eugénie, the beautiful and elegant wife of Napoleon III, brought the first one—in grey, with black lace and pink bows—to England when, in April 1855, she and the Emperor visited Queen Victoria at Windsor. So universally was it adopted that it earned its inventor almost a million francs in less than a month because, in the words of Peter Quennell, it liberated women from being encased in 'several layers of petticoat, starched muslin, corded calico, thick flannel, while a

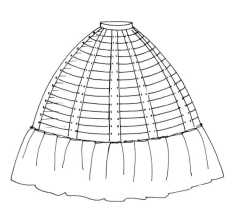

Crinoline made of vertical bands of tape with rows of steel stiffening and pleated flounce c.1858

Crinoline with flat front and wide ruched back, but no springs c.1865

roll of plaited horsehair beneath the outer petticoat ensured the proper degree of solidity and amplitude'.

This crinoline remained in fashion until about 1865, by which time its shape had begun to change. The front became flatter and the great sweep of skirt flowed out behind instead of all round. By 1870 this backward trend led to the crinoline being replaced by the bustle.

The crinoline was subject to all the disadvantages of the earlier eighteenth-century hoops, and these were multiplied by the fact that, unlike the hooped skirt, the crinoline spread to all classes. It was worn by factory workers, and caused havoc where china, glass or other breakable goods were being manufactured. A German critic of 1865 noted peasant girls working in fields in crinolines. Among many disadvantages it was difficult to manoeuvre it in and out of carriages and it took up a great amount of space in rooms, where it made sitting down a problem. It was disastrous to trip or fall when wearing it, because the whole contraption could come over the wearer's head, with embarrassing and ludicrous results, and in this event it was extremely difficult for her to right herself.

There is an account of a disaster of this kind at the beginning of Arnold Bennett's *Old Wives' Tale,* when the two young girls, Sophia and Constance, unpack their mother's newly delivered crinoline and Sophia tries it on: 'Her mother's tremendous new gown ballooned about her in all its fantastic richness and expensiveness'. But disaster soon followed: 'Then Sophia fell, in stepping backwards; the pyramid was overbalanced, great distended rings of silk trembled and swayed gigantically on the floor, and Sophia's small feet lay like the feet of a doll on the rim of the largest circle, which curved and arched above them like a cavern's mouth . . . .

The girls regained their feet, Sophia with Constance's help. It was not easy to right a capsized crinoline'.

A new item of underwear at this time was the camisole, a short bodice worn over the corset, mainly to keep that garment clean. It was at first often called a waistcoat. This same mid-century period saw the arrival of various styles of bust improvers, ranging from pads to what were called 'lemon bosoms'. Devices of this kind were to continue for almost the whole of the century in a variety of forms. Even today, when most earlier items of underwear have either become obsolete or been transformed beyond all recognition, the shape of the bosom is still quite frequently 'improved' by means of wiring or padding built into the bra. The full story of the brassière was not, however, to unfold until the end of the nineteenth century.

The dominating 'improvement' to which the figure was subjected in the nineteenth century was the habit of tight-lacing. Throughout the previous four hundred years of fashion history the narrow waist had been the pivot of all the changing styles, except those of the brief French Revolution era in the years round the turn of the eighteenth to the nineteenth century. The main function of the corset had been to emphasise the waist, by subjecting the body to pressure at that point, often with a severity and to a degree that today are almost incomprehensible. Tight-lacing was practised by the fashionable in most epochs; to what extent and by what proportion of other women it is hard to assess today. But in the nineteenth century it seems to have been more prevalent than ever before and to have been pursued with a relentless assiduity.

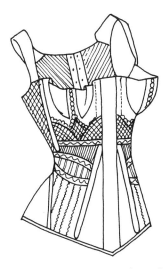

Strong cotton stays, boned and stitched, with wide front busk c.1830

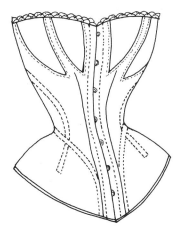

Front fastening corset with patent clips c. 1862

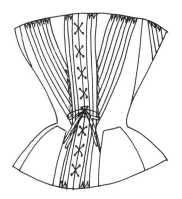

Boned corset in blue silk c.1864

Tight-lacing was the centre of a storm of controversy throughout the middle part of the century. Its supporters and its enemies voiced their views at great length from pre-crinoline days onwards. 'The subject of tight-lacing' says Janet Dunbar, 'raged through the newspapers and journals of the forties and fifties' and the fury increased in the sixties and seventies.

A fervent and highly eloquent, not to say highly-coloured, defence of it came in a book *The Corset and the Crinoline* by W. B. L. (William Barry Lord), which was published in 1868 and received considerable attention. Although sub-titled 'A book of modes and costumes from remote periods to the present time', it defines its purpose in the preface as to 'do our best to lay clearly before our readers the historical facts—experiences and arguments—relating to the much discussed "corset question" '—which means tight-lacing. With this purpose the admitted strictures of contemporary writers on the damage to health caused by the tight corset are swept aside in a fiery diatribe against the reckless attack on 'the stays by the aid of which their wives and daughters are made presentable in society'.

After this the book makes it evident that the ruling purpose of its 224 pages is to justify tight-lacing in all the rigours under which it was practised in the nineteenth century. The arguments for the corset-narrowed waist are built up from pre-history and are diligently assembled age by age to prove that the custom has had world-wide, centuries-long approval. Included among the examples of the tight-lacing cult are Java, Ceylon, the South Seas, Tartary, Circassia, Ancient Egypt, India, Persia, Old Testament Palestine, legendary Greece and the Roman Empire. Lavish illustrations demonstrate the hour-glass figure in many of these places.

After skirting over the 'long weird night of mental darkness . . . from the tenth to the middle of the fifteenth century' when waists were not provable, the chronicle resumes its praise of the narrow-corseted waist through the ensuing eras, but reserves its main attention for a defence of the cult of tight-lacing as practised in the nineteenth century, mainly at the time of writing.

Then follow profuse references to contemporary views on the subject of tight-lacing, together with numerous extracts from the 'vast number of letters and papers touching the use of the Corset' which had been appearing in leading ladies' magazines over many years. It is impossible not to view with some scepticism the 'facts' proclaimed in these letters to the editor, but even if some of the evidence is contrived, consciously or otherwise, the fact that it secured publication at such length in leading periodicals must carry weight.

In 1810, it is recalled, tight-lacing had been 'revived with a degree of fury . . . which posterity will not credit. Stays are now composed, not of whalebone, indeed, or hardened leather, but of bars of iron and steel from three to four inches broad and many of them not less than eighteen in length'. It was not unusual at this time to see 'a mother lay her daughter down upon the carpet, and, placing her foot on her back, break half-a-dozen laces in tightening her stays'. This at the height of the 'freedom' era!

Of such severity the author does not approve, but he puts forward the plea that if tight-lacing is started early enough in life it will not cause such tortures and that modern, lighter corsets are less oppressive. An example of the gentle persuasion of the waist into slimness is that of a girl who became a pupil at a 'West-End School' at the age of thirteen and was on arrival fitted with corsets which 'did not open in front and were fastened by the under-governess in such a manner that to attempt to unlace them during the night would be immediately detected at the morning's inspection. After the first week or two she felt no discomfort or pain of any kind, though, as she was still growing, her stays became proportionately tighter'.

In reply to the argument that tight-lacing is injurious to the health, many vehement letters are quoted from ladies who boast of sixteen-inch waists and perfect health, including one, published in the *Queen*, urging blandly that 'if the various organs are prevented from taking a certain form or direction, they will accommodate themselves to any other with perfect ease'.

In the *Englishwoman's Domestic Magazine* early in 1868 another correspondent, who had not laced tightly until she was married, is put on record as telling how she started doing so because her husband was 'so particularly fond of a small waist'. Although her waist was twenty-three inches, she ordered a fourteen-inch pair of stays, and 'managed the first day to lace my waist in to eighteen inches'. Sleeping in her corset at night, she got her maid to tighten it one inch each day, until the laces met and her waist was fourteen inches. 'For the first few days the pain was very great . . . but in a month or so I would not have taken them off on any account'. By her husband's admiration she was 'amply repaid for my trouble'.

One protesting voice is quoted—a girl who was one of forty or fifty pupils 'daily imprisoned on vices of whalebone drawn tight by the muscular arms of sturdy waiting-maids . . . all entreaties were vain, as no relaxation of the cruel laces was allowed during the day under any pretext except decided illness'. The result was that the muscles were so weakened that the unfortunate girl had to keep on lacing tightly as 'her muscles were powerless to support her'.

This produced storms of protest from fervent advocates of tight-lacing including schoolmistresses, who, evidently of a very different character from those of more recent generations, rushed into the fray in defence of tight-lacing. One of them even brushes aside the earlier writer's complaints about her sufferings on the grounds that she had admitted that 'she did not experience any inconvenience after the first two years'. Another claims that tight-lacing is justified because it only makes girls 'temporary sufferers'.

Needless to say, the other side of the story also found many eloquent advocates. The cudgels were taken up very firmly in *Madra Natura Versus the Moloch of Fashion. A Social Essay* by Luke Limner (John Leighton), published in 1874. He sets out 'to pourtray the pernicious effects of a grand social error', and from describing the terrible fate of the 'victims destroyed by wearing hoops and crinolines' which frequently catch fire, he continues to claim that 'we cannot but think it very justifiable to consider these 'confectionneurs' of 'Corsets' as a race of most mischievous mountebanks.'

Spiegel, an eminent doctor and anatomist, is cited as having imputed, in all seriousness, the greatly increased mortality in England among the females of the upper classes, from consumption and diseases of the chest, 'to the general use of stays'. The effect of the corset is declared 'to portend an ultimate decay of the physical organism of the individuals of the upper classes of society.' Medical men all over Europe are quoted as having 'raised their voices in stern reprehension of, and admonition against, a custom that annually exhibited a greater amount of victims self-immolated to the Moloch of Fashion than had ever been imagined'. Doctors have, moreover, published from time to time records of 'the frightful amount of physical suffering, of diseases, deformity and premature death resulting from stays'. To crown his account of all that was seen and recorded of dire calamity from 1857 to 1864 during the so-called 'Crinoline mania', he compiles a list three and a half printed pages long of the diseases and maladies caused by tight-lacing.

Concluding that 'many long years, and many yet unborn generations must pass away before the female mind in the upper and wealthier classes of society in this country will believe that the grace and beauty of form of nature are best', he strikes a modern note by urging better education for girls, including a knowledge of medicine, and by pointing out that 'exercise and diet are the only hindrances to embonpoint'.

A revealing footnote to these and a host of other accounts of Victorian tight-lacing has been provided in our time by Doris Langley Moore, a leading costume expert. In order to find out the facts about the reputed eighteen-inch waist, she measured more than 1000 waisted women's costumes from the Victorian period. She failed to find any less than 20½ inches round. The Gallery of English Costume, Manchester, bears out her findings: it has no dress on show that measures less than 21 inches at the waistline. To minimise measurements is an enduring and not wholly un-endearing vanity—did the Victorians indulge in self-delusion about their waists in the way that many substantial ladies of today will, without batting an eyelid, declare themselves size twelve and never, never admit to being a self-evident sixteen?

5 | *The Dawn of Freedom:*
1840–1880

Corset with long curved front-fastening busk c.1879

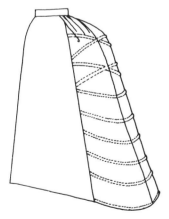

Striped twill bustle, back stiffened with whalebone c.1885

From the mid-nineteenth century the corset continued to change in shape and construction to a considerable extent, just as did the outer fashions to which it lent much of their form. Up to the 1840's corsets still had shoulder straps and at that time they also had pronounced rounded cup-shaped bust sections. Gussets were also inserted to shape hips and busts.

The shaping of corsets by joining up separate pieces instead of by adding gussets to one-piece garments began in the late 1840's and became very popular in the eighteen-fifties. Cording and quilting were also in vogue, and the corset was sometimes worn over the crinoline and petticoats, so as to achieve the smallest possible waist. In colour white was the most elegant choice, but grey, putty, red and black were also used for practical reasons.

Corsets still came high above the waist and throughout the crinoline era—from the 1850's to the late 1860's—they still contained the bosom. The stiff front busk was a continuing feature and it lasted during the time when the front fastening, introduced in the early 1830's, gradually ousted complete dependence upon back lacing as the only way of putting on or taking off the corset.

In the late 1860's another contribution was made to the strict shaping of the corset by the introduction of steam-moulding. This meant that the corset, when stitched together and made up, with its busk and bones, was heavily starched and dried and stiffened by being placed on a steam mould made in the desired shape. It therefore became 'set' in its shape. One of these moulds still exists at Symington's corset collection at Market Harborough. It is a hollow copper shape, fixed to a bench, and the steam was 'fed' into it from a series of pipes running under the bench and up into the mould.

From being a vast circular bell the crinoline in the later 1860's gradually became flatter in front and concentrated its build-up of the figure on the back. At the same time skirts began to be looped up lavishly behind, revealing a considerable amount of petticoat. By this means the crinoline evolved into the bustle. By 1870 the fashionable outline showed a horizontal projection at the back, supported either by below-waist petticoat flounces or by whalebones inserted into the petticoat or by a separate 'basket' of whalebone, cane or steel attached at the waist between the petticoat and the dress. This was known as a crinolette. 'The crinoline projected hideously at the side, whereas the crinolette will only stick out at the back', commented *The World* in July 1881. It was even said that a tea tray could be laid safely on this projection, so wide did it sometimes become! With these bustles the front of the dress was drawn tightly back across the figure from waist to knee level, often by means of tapes.

In the eighteen-eighties, when the figure was being increasingly revealed in front by the eclipse of the crinoline and the intermittent comings and goings of the bustle in its various forms, corsets became heavier and longer. The spoon busk appeared and great numbers of whalebones were used. One corset of the early 1880's has twenty separate shaped pieces and on each side there are sixteen whalebones. The increasing elegance of corsets and the skill put into their construction were an encouragement to dressmakers to shape skirts more closely to the figure than they would otherwise have dared and in the 1880's the variety of bustles was immense.

One, which seemed in name at least to be in line with a coming trend in outer clothing and underwear, was what an advertisement described as 'the braided wire health bustle, warranted to be less heating to the spine than any others.' Health had not hitherto been a pre-requisite of underwear. Lily Langtry gave her name to another bustle of the time, described by James Laver as 'an arrangement of metal bands working on a pivot. It could be raised when sitting down and sprang back automatically when the lady rose to her feet! One of the most extraordinary inventions in the whole history of fashion.'

Petticoats became increasingly elaborate and after the invention of chemical dyes in the 1860's they also became extremely colourful. A fashion book produced by Debenham & Freebody for the autumn of 1874 states, in notes relating to underclothing, that 'In Petticoats one of the best patterns for day wear has a deep kilted flounce all round, wheels of embroidery appearing on the outside of each plait; it has the advantage of ironing easily. For evening wear they are made very long and elaborately trimmed with plaitings, lace and embroidery. There are various new arrangements of stiff skirts for

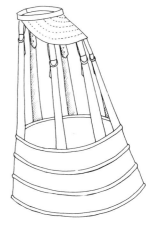

Red flannel crinoline c.1869 with flat front

Longcloth under-petticoat with stiffly starched muslin frills c.1873

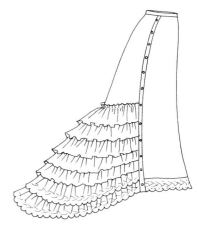

Under-skirt with frilled train c.1879

*1870 crinolette with steels,
back lacing and flat front
with buttons*

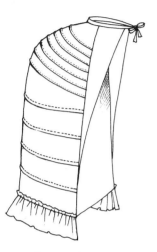

*Bustle in red cotton satin
c.1875*

evening wear. Among the best are those made in check muslin, buttoning down the front and having a series of flounces at the back, under the two upper ones of which are tape runners that draw them together, and make them more bouffante. In addition to this, a double puff of the cross-cut muslin, is made to button on at the waist, so as to iron more easily.

'The washing steel suitable for all climates is a spécialité to be highly recommended. The newest Crinolettes from Paris are made of red Cashmere, they button down the front, but have only steels at the back; their peculiar feature being, that, in addition to the usual steels in tape-runners, they have outside these a series of red Cashmere flounces edged with steel.'

These are awe-inspiring details, but there was no end to the elaborations of the petticoats of the last twenty years of the nineteenth century. A pink satin petticoat of the 1880's is more than four yards wide at the hem, above which it is lined and stiffened. Deep folds at the back draw the fullness there. All but the main seams are hand-sewn, including all the frills. A purple satin quilted petticoat of the same time has the same back pleats. Another is in quilted Paisley pattern, and one in black taffeta has a long train and is entirely hand-sewn. All these are included in the Museum of Costume at Bath.

In addition to quilted petticoats for warmth, many were made of flannel. Red flannel came to the fore in 1880, and was 'believed to have some special efficacy in keeping out chills, and the most elegant

*Fine lawn petticoat, trimmed
with tucks and lace, 1890's*

*Quilted petticoat of 1880's
in Paisley printed cotton*

Corset cover in red flannel, 1880's

Red flannel petticoat of 1880's with shaped yoke in natural cotton

as well as the humblest women wore it', but it was used prior to that. A red flannel crinoline with four steel hoops is included in the collection at Snowshill Manor.

In 1873, the year of the marriage of the Prince of Wales, later Edward VII, to Princess Alexandra of Denmark, the Princess petticoat made its appearance. Combining camisole or bodice and petticoat in a one-piece garment and originally buttoning down the back, it was a tribute to the beautiful and elegant wife of the heir to Victoria's throne. The Princess was, however, not the inventor of it, any more than Wellington invented the boot called after him. (But Lily Langtry, the Jersey lily, did start the fashion for the woven material known ever since as jersey. Also Lord Cardigan, after standing with his back to the fire and burning his coat tails, cut off the tails and thereby introduced the casual short jacket which was henceforth to be called after him. Lord Raglan originated the sleeve called after him and Lord Spencer was the source of the spencer).

Corsets, like the rest of underwear, became more decorative in the 1880's and were sometimes made of satin with deep lace at the top. Many colours were used, including yellow, apricot and deep blue. To keep the bones in position embroidery was frequently used, with designs often representing flowers in a variety of colours. Patterns of this embroidery still exist.

An important innovation at this time was the first suspender. James Laver records that in 1876 Grand Opera Bouffe, with music by Offenbach, was presented at the Alhambra Theatre, Leicester Square,

Harness-type suspenders c. 1880

Suspenders on waist belt c. 1886

Corset with attached suspenders c.1901

and great excitement was roused by French dancers with 'naked thighs with suspenders stretched across them to keep up the stockings.' By 1878 these suspenders were being worn in Britain in real life. They were originally attached to a separate kind of harness and later to a belt, both worn over the corset, and it was not until 1901 that they were attached to the corset. They were a double boon, not only replacing restricting garters but also anchoring the corset so that it could be longer and more shapely. Eventually, too, suspenders made it possible for the corset to be less constricting. As they kept it in place and prevented it from riding up, the waist did not have to be so desperately tight in order to achieve this result.

In the early 1880's the bustle, instead of being a waist-high projection, had evolved into a cluster of draped material below the hipline at the back. Above it the dress followed the figure to this point more closely than it had done for centuries. The fullness of petticoats was sometimes pulled away from the front by the further aid of draw-strings. There was, however, a brief return of the high projecting bustle in the later 1880's, when it was combined with a very tight, flat front from throat to hem.

Underwear in general began to be modernised in order to accommodate these styles, but for most of the nineteenth century its main characteristic, and the oddest to our eyes, was its voluminousness. Chemises of the early nineteenth century are huge. They have enormously wide necklines, caught in by drawstrings, and wide sleeves, often also pulled in at the elbow. Frequently there were additional pieces inserted at the top of the sleeves, and these were flattened by minute pleating given to them in the ironing. The sleeve was still a straight piece of material with a large under-arm gusset to make movement possible.

Typical good quality chemises of the mid-nineteenth century are made of extremely fine linen, almost of a handkerchief-like texture. The sewing, still, of course, by hand, is meticulously fine and impeccably neat, both inside and out. The size of the garments, the amount of elaboration in the cutting of sleeves and yokes and the extent of fine tucking makes them remarkable. One young lady is on record as having spent a month sewing and embroidering one undergarment.

From the 1860's chemises started to become more attractive. Broderie anglaise was used to edge the neck and sleeves, which were shorter. Later in the century lace edging and rows of lace insertion appeared. Sleeves sometimes were absent, the armholes being finished by a row of lace or broderie anglaise. Necklines became less wide and the tighter neck was fastened by means of a button on a short front opening. Sometimes the garments became rather shorter—above knee-length—but for many years after the half-century they were still immensely wide and often long enough to reach the calves of the average woman. By the mid-seventies the chemise was being shaped to the waist below the bust, so as to make it less bulky and conform to the flatter line of waist and hips in outer clothes.

It is a curious fact that the Victorians, usually regarded as a by-word for dreary practicality in underwear, were in fact innovators in the introduction of finer materials, trimmings of lace and embroidery and were also the first to introduce silk as an underwear material. This was in the 1880's. 'Underclothing is now made in soft silk and is as much trimmed with lace as our dresses, with hand embroidery most beautifully done,' said *Sylvia's Home Journal* in 1880. By the end of the century wool was worn for warmth, but for fashion, 'fine lawn, muslin and silk, trimmed with lace and embroidery and threaded with ribbons, had become still more decorated and more decorative' says Anne Buck, an authority on Victorian costume.

Drawers were by the 1880's in general wear, and they shared with chemises the outstanding property of being enormous in size.

Knee-length cotton chemise edged with eyelet-embroidery c.1866

*White cotton open knickers
with back fastening c.1860*

Examples in the collection at the Victoria and Albert Museum give the impression, as do the chemises, of being made for giantesses. They are two or three times as large as would seem necessary or desirable.

The design of drawers, from the 1860's until the early years of the twentieth century, still consists of two almost separate sections, one for each leg, joined only just below the waist, where they are gathered on to a substantial band. They are therefore open from below-waist to the edge of the leg. Sometimes drawers are cut entirely on the cross, at others large godets are added to the opening at the back, so that the two sides can overlap voluminously. These garments usually fasten at the waistband, crossing over at the back, with tapes going round the waist to secure them.

One example at the Victoria and Albert Museum carries the monogram VR and belongs to the 1860's. It has the usual open back and the waistband has tapes which cross over at the back. The legs are straight, with rows of minute tucks to decorate them. The material is very fine linen and the sewing is so minute as to be almost invisible.

About 1877 a new undergarment appeared, the first of a whole series that were to proliferate from then into the following century and in so doing to transform underwear and help to produce an entirely new concept of it. This novelty was combinations. They combined chemise and drawers in one garment and were at first made in the same linen and cotton materials, and also at times of flannel and merino. Their attraction was that they reduced the bulk of the underwear and therefore helped the trend of outer fashion towards bodices that followed the figure closely down to the bottom of the hips—a trend not seen for centuries. The main development of combinations came, however, considerably later and falls mainly into the early part of the present century. But during the last quarter of the nineteenth century they jostled quite actively with the traditional chemise and drawers for a place in the underwear wardrobe.

The cult of slimness, which they would have aided, was not showing any signs of capturing fashion, and the vogue of the times was for the other extreme. The ideal, laid down in 1873 as the taste of the time, declared that 'a well-developed bust, a tapering waist and large hips are the combination of points recognised as a good figure'—and that lasted for more than thirty years, during which the mature beauty with a flamboyant figure reigned supreme, for the last time.

The bust, as at certain previous times and at all periods since then to our own day, was provided with artificial aids to curvaciousness when nature failed. With the lengthening of corsets to ensure becomingly flowing hips these garments became correspondingly lower above the waist. The under-bodice or camisole, introduced to cover the gap, and gaining steadily in popularity and elegance, was not an effective shape-maker. There were, however, plenty of additional remedies available.

Jaconet under-bodice c.1876

In the mid-nineteenth century a French firm advertised *poitrines adhérentes* of pink rubber, which were described as following the movements of respiration with perfect precision. In 1860 a patent was obtained for an improved inflated undulating artificial bust' to augment the female figure. Other devices followed in continuous succession, including numerous styles and sizes of bust pads, celluloid and rubber bust shapes and 'lemon bosoms'.

There were also, in the 1880's, camisole-like garments with elaborate structures of whalebone or a series of wire springs built into the underside of the front. By adjusting certain tapes these could produce an 'improved' bust of selected dimensions. It was a feature of these that there was a complete absence of any division or of the much-sought-after 'cleavage' of later times. The bust was a rounded bolster, providing, perhaps with more comfort than later, Browning's dream of 'the breast's supurb abundance where a man might lay his head.'

Bust bodice, boned and taped to give rounded effect c.1890

These new garments that gave artificial shape to the bust were the first bust bodices, forerunners of an article of underwear which by the early twentieth century was to be one of the most important of all, probably second only to the corset in its influence on fashion. And though its history covers only about eighty years, it has in that time gone through as many changes and variations as has corsetry in all its centuries.

While to all appearances nineteenth-century fashion was pursuing a course that, as has just been shown, was familiar, and continuous with previous history, immense forces of change in fashion were increasingly at work beneath the surface throughout at least the whole second half of the century. In certain respects their direct origins dated back earlier than that. Much later, within the first quarter of the twentieth century, all these disparate forces were to

Heavily boned bust bodice c.1890

coalesce and start actively erupting in a revolution in all aspects of women's dress, outer and inner, which has gone on ever since and still shows no signs of reverting to any bygone pattern.

It would be unnatural and a freakish coincidence if it did so. Fashion, however insignificant it is in relation to the tremendous scientific discoveries and cosmic conquests of our time, is inevitably part of this age. Its nature is to accommodate itself to the world in which spacesuits have become a more natural part of the clothes story than crinolines and bustles.

Several separate and radically unconnected factors were to contribute to the beginnings of the fashion revolution of today which in the event has transformed underwear even more than outer clothes. These new factors made their first appearances at different periods and in different circumstances, so they must be considered separately if their total combined effect is to be assessed in a coherent way.

The primary and most important contribution to fashion change was also the earliest to start. It was the emancipation of women and it is still going on. But there is one apparently very odd fact about the 'woman's movement.' It began early in the nineteenth century and might even be said with some justification to have originated in Mary Wollestonecraft's *Vindication of the Rights of Woman,* published in 1792. It began to achieve practical results with the passing of the Infants' Custody Bill in 1839, the first result of the redoubtable efforts of Mrs. Caroline Norton to secure recognition of the human rights of the female half of the human race. It showed its rising momentum in the Marriage & Divorce Act of 1857 and in the Married Women's Property Acts of 1881 (Scotland) and 1882 (England, Wales and Ireland).

The forces of women's emancipation were active in many directions by the middle years of the century, and John Stuart Mill advocated women's suffrage in 1861 in his book 'Representative Government'. But this had at first no effect on the fashions that women wore. The tyranny of tight-lacing, crinolines, bustles, voluminous petticoats, constricting underwear and skirts that trailed on the ground went side by side for many years with the activities by which women sought freedom not only by the vote but also in the right to higher education, to careers, to entry into such professions as medicine and law. In short, the right to a stake in the way the society they lived in was run.

They sought freedom, but they remained enslaved to fashions deriving from the eras they decried. They continued to look outwardly like the contemporary versions of the leisured and idle women who had always been the arbiters of fashion. 'It was', records Ray Strachey, writing on the women's movement, 'in black silk gowns, corsets, crinolines and elastic-sided boots that these intrepid ladies began to turn society out . . . and in ladylike fashion they succeeded'. There were a few murmurs of protest; George Eliot, for instance, wrote of her youthful revolt against the tight-lacing enjoined by a governess acting in the spirit of the times. But in general there was acceptance of the established traditions and conventions of fashion.

It might be argued that at this point, the mid-sixties and seventies of last century, the call for emancipation was being voiced by only a minority of women and that therefore the general trend of fashion would not immediately be affected. High fashion and high thinking are not natural soul-mates and fashion had its roots centuries-deep as against the new woman's few years of active campaigning.

There probably is some element of truth in this, but there was a far stronger reason for what seems an inexplicable lagging of fashion in the rear of the course of women's progress. The pioneers of women's rights were acutely aware that their demands would be regarded by the majority of men and women as an enormity. The women themselves would therefore be expected to look freakish, to dress with a wild disregard for the conventions, with grotesque eccentricity, lack of care or outright mannishness.

To counter irrelevant strictures on their appearance, which would obscure their serious inner purpose, the women who were pioneering for recognition as citizens made it almost a point of honour to conform strictly to the accepted fashions of their time. When the *Englishwoman's Journal* was set up in 1857 as the voice of the new movement, a prospective helper described how, on visiting its offices in Bloomsbury, she expected 'to see some dowdy old lady, and found herself in the midst of young women who were well dressed, beautiful and gay.'

When a special meeting of the Social Science Association, the liberalising organisation favouring women's progress and founded by F. D. Maurice, was held in 1866 as part of the drive to obtain official permission for girls to take the Oxford and Cambridge Local Examinations, Miss Emily Davies, a pioneer of the women's movement, made special arrangements for 'some well-dressed and good-looking young women to fill up the front row', in order to refute the idea of plain, dreary 'blue-stockings'.

When, in the 1870's, women were again undertaking the then pioneer activity of addressing meetings all over Britain on the subject of the much-sought-after parliamentary vote, it was noted that 'when an audience expected to find a fierce and strident virago, and found instead a young lady whose voice, dress and manner were not only quiet but exquisite, then indeed they were startled to attention.'

When women students first established themselves at Lady Margaret Hall, Oxford, as a result of the Enabling Act of 1878, which opened the universities to women, there was great anxiety that the first students should 'dress carefully and have gentle manners'. All the conventions were meticulously maintained, with chaperonage observed as strictly as at the most conventional levels of the society whose shackles these pioneer women were bent on breaking.

The conventions of dress even defeated Mrs. Amelia Bloomer, the American writer and journalist, who visited England in 1851 in an endeavour to promote rational clothing for women in the shape of the garments which were called after her. She eventually discarded 'bloomers' herself because she feared lest the furore they had created and the jokes they had provoked would kill her genuine and deserved reputation as a serious writer.

Yet her idea was not in fact so extreme—a normal fitted bodice of the time, with a below-knee-length skirt, full but not stiffened, and underneath it baggy drawers or trousers caught in at the ankle and usually ending in a lace frill. But 'excitement, ridicule, vituperation' were provoked, as James Laver records. Dozens of Punch cartoons appeared and the idea of women trying 'to wear the trousers' raised a storm. It was not until nearly fifty years later that Mrs. Bloomer's innovation became, comparatively peaceably, an accepted reality. Bloomers then became a description of an outer garment and also, well into the twentieth century, of a style of loose, closed knickers caught in below or above the knee with elastic and worn both by young girls and adult women, especially for games and sport.

It is tempting to connect the opening up of physical activities to women with their political struggles for recognition, but it is very doubtful if this has any real validity, although undoubtedly the two contributed to each other's progress. The health cult, which gathered great force from the eighteen-eighties, was a far wider movement, involving both men and women of every class and degree. It profoundly affected the outer dress and underwear of the whole community and was part of a dawning new outlook on life and on the whole structure of society.

The new freedom in clothes began to come to men many years before women felt its effects, although ultimately it was to have more effect on women's attire than that of men—naturally, because their clothing had so much further to go before it became 'rationalised' in the sense of allowing freedom of movement and comfort in whatever activities were undertaken.

In Gainsborough's portraits, notably that of Mr. & Mrs. Andrews (1748) and The Morning Walk (1785) it is noticeable that while the man in each couple wears relatively practical outdoor dress, the women are dressed as if for the most formal of indoors occasions. Mrs. Andrews, with fashionably immense panniers on her pale blue silk dress, could be attired for a ball but for her hat, while the elaborate, sophisticated dress of the walking lady is adorned with ruffles galore, and she also wears a towering flowered and feathered picture hat. Did they, one wonders, miss some of the pleasure of the countryside by approaching it so formally—like the later lady in Frances Cornford's poem:

> *Why do you walk through the fields in gloves,*
> *Missing so much and so much?*

By the 1830's practical walking dress had become usual for men, but it was not until thirty years later that women's fashionable clothes showed any distinction between what was suitable for the drawing room and for the country. There was, perhaps, very little need for such distinction. *Fraser's Magazine* in the 1830's says that girls' schools had no playgrounds and the only exercise was walks along the public roads two by two. The *Westminster Review* in 1849–50 declares that 'girls would be thought mad to run, leap or engage in any kind of active game in the open fields'.

In 1874 opponents of women's suffrage put forward the argument that the female physique was inadequate to cope with the responsibilities involved. The rejoinder of women to this curious qualification for the vote was that little or no chance was given to girls to develop a proper physique. The strong plea for physical exercise that this promoted resulted in games beginning to be introduced into girls' schools of the enlightened kind that were springing up about this time. The effect of this innovation gradually influenced the clothes girls wore for these new-found activities— and this involved underwear quite as much as outer apparel.

By the 1880's women's walking dress had made a big leap forward and had become a tailor-made, worn with knickerbockers and what was described as 'sanitary underclothing'. This included wool next to the skin—a new cult—and though corsets were still worn and the waist sharply defined, petticoats were reduced to one or even none. The novel knickerbockers, at first worn under a skirt, were the first closed knickers to be worn, and had a buttoned flap at the back. The tailored jacket and skirt were new and revolutionary, even though the skirt still clung round the ankles and the sportswoman was still gloved and hatted. For some reason these walking outfits were usually made of extremely heavy material, such as tweed or serge, and in dark colours. Progress had still far to go.

But there was now, for the first time, a dual wardrobe, and a dual set of underwear. The traditional elaborate undergarments continued to be worn for ordinary social life, with elaborate dresses. But flannel vests, woollen combinations and the new knickerbockers were donned for the new habit of exercise. In the 1880's young ladies were actually going on walking holidays and the gentle activity of croquet was being superseded by the innovation of lawn tennis, still, of course, played in long skirts, hats and gloves but nevertheless a landmark in progress.

The sportsgirl of the 1880's seems to us today almost as remote from reality as the women in the earlier fashion pageants of farthingales, panniers, crinolines and bustles, but the advance was immense from the long-term view. Stiffening and whalebone, frills, flounces and furbelows had gone from at least one part of women's wardrobes. The tailor-made was, astoundingly, made by a man's tailor, and women were exchanging their traditional elaborate hats for caps like men's, for stiff man-style straw boaters and even for deerstalkers. They were beginning to wear blouses based on the style of a man's shirt, complete with high collar and tie.

For the moment—in the eighteen-eighties—this revolution naturally resulted in a diversity of underwear. Vests and combinations vied for popularity with the former chemise, and gradually won the day. Vests were made of merino, silk and wool; sometimes they were coloured and one at least exists in plum-coloured stockinette.

The relaxation in women's underwear was echoed at this time in that of young girls. Throughout history until the latter part of the nineteenth century even very small girls were dressed as miniature grown-ups. Constricting corsets and tight-lacing, as has already been recorded, were advocated for even the preteens in the crinoline era. But from about 1880 there was a gradual change and young people began to have their own kind of clothes.

A stayband had traditionally been worn from babyhood by both sexes, for warmth as well as support, though it was dropped in fairly early years in the case of boys. It took many forms and was made in depths varying from 3 inches to 14 inches. The most usual style was a flat, unshaped stiff band made of red or grey cloth on the outside, with an interlining of hessian and a white lining. The band was usually also corded, for firmness, and the more luxurious ones were quilted with a layer of wadding between the outside and the lining. There were cut-out underarms and tape straps going over the shoulders. These bands were either buttoned in front or fastened there with a large hook and eye.

From the age of about ten girls wore a more shaped type of bodice, but one of similar construction, corded or boned. A modified version of this continued to be worn during the first quarter of the present century, but its popularity was waning. The big breakaway came in the appropriately named Liberty bodice, introduced by the corset firm of Symington in 1908. A soft knitted garment, with nothing more formidable than bands of tape to keep it in shape, it was quite simply a front-buttoning bodice. In a few years it became world-famous, ousting the old restricting stay-bands, and bodices, and the output of it rose steadily year by year to an annual 3,500,000. In 1923 a light-weight version, the 'Peter Pan' fleecy bodice, was added, and was also very successful.

The Liberty bodice was part and parcel of the normal young girl's underwear for nearly half a century, and many middle-aged and elderly women of today can recall wearing it. It is still manufactured in substantial quantities and it continued to be quite widely worn until the late fifties, when manufacturers began to cater for the teenager's increasingly sophisticated tastes by designing young ranges of bras, suspender belts and, more recently, pantees, all specially styled for the adolescent, growing figure.

6 | *Health and Sport: 1880 – 1905*

A new note was introduced into the underwear of both men and women in the 1880's by another movement which was to have effects as important as political emancipation on the daily lives of women of all classes. This was the application of health principles to clothing, and especially to underclothing.

'Wool next to the skin' was one of the rules of life for a large proportion of the populace from the 'eighties and 'nineties of last century until the development of man-made fibres after the Second World War. It is still widely held. The cult did not creep in haphazardly and the immense effect it had on the underwear of men, women and children was no mere whim of fashion. The man who assailed the centuries-old acceptance of the cotton chemise or shirt, with a limited use of flannel, usually rough and of mixed origin, was Dr. Gustav Jaeger, M.D., Professor of Zoology and Physiology at the University of Stuttgart, author of a number of books on health culture and originator of Dr. Jaeger's Sanitary Woollen System, which made an immense impact on the development of underwear not only in Germany but all over Europe and not least in Britain.

His first book, a collection of essays on health culture, was published in Germany in 1878 and was based on ten years' study of the subject of clothing and its effect on health. He testified that he cured his own chronic ill-health, excess of weight, indigestion and various other ailments by the wearing of wool clothing. This procedure revealed that 'stomach, heart, lungs and brain all show greater vitality.' His wife and children also responded to the 'cure' of wool clothing for various ailments and infections. He himself became able to garden for several hours without strain, an activity previously resulting in exhaustion, and a woollen collar cured a hoarse voice which had interfered with 'my chief pleasure in sitting down at home to the piano and singing a song.' Not only was he cured but 'my daughter remarked that my voice sounded plainer and clearer than ever' and later 'my voice had attained an increased compass.'

The principle behind Dr. Jaeger's theory was that only animal fibres prevented the retention of the 'noxious exhalations' of the body, retained the salutary emanations of the body which induce a sense of vigour and sound health and ensured warmth and ventilation. But it had to be wool and wool alone that was worn. Even pockets and linings must be of wool. Handkerchiefs were to be woollen ones, hats likewise, and boots had to have wool inserted in them. All bedding had to be of wool.

The subject of health was beginning to attract attention everywhere at this time, but the impact Dr. Jaeger's clothing made in Britain was due to one man. This was Mr. L. R. S. Tomalin, manager of a wholesale grocery firm in the City of London. So impressed was he by reading one of Dr. Jaeger's books that he secured the sole rights to the use of the Jaeger name, publications and system, patents, trade marks, etc. in Great Britain, with a view to developing the ideas that so impressed him. He also had a huge bonfire in his garden for all the non-woollen clothing and bed-linen possessed by his household. Mr. Tomalin forthwith broke away from his previous occupation and on February 1st 1884 started manufacturing Jaeger clothing, all of it 100% pure wool, in a small way in premises in Fore Street, in the City. The business made rapid progress and in the autumn of 1884 won a gold medal for its stand at 'The Healtheries'—the International Health Exhibition held in London. In October of the same year the venture received the accolade of a long leader page article in *The Times* on the new Jaeger idea that we should all wear wool or other animal fibre clothing. 'A new gospel', *The Times* declared, 'has reached us . . . it is a medical theory, based on the close observations of animal life, demonstrated by scientific experiments, and proved by practical experience . . . the evidence in its favour is sufficiently strong and the success achieved so widespread that it is, at least, only right to state the case, leaving the public, in Dr. Jaeger's own words, free to examine everything and retain the best.'

In February 1884 the *Lancet* congratulated Dr. Jaeger 'on his able and practical recognition of the usefulness of wool as a covering' and in August of that year the *British Medical Journal* referred to the skill of the new adaptation of animal wool 'as a sanitary substitute in articles hitherto manufactured of other materials.' Doctors testified by the hundred to the relief from rheumatism due to the sanitary woollen system.

After this Fore Street became thronged with carriages from the

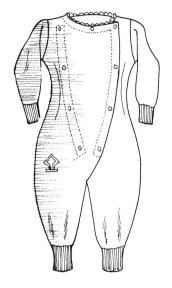

Dr. Jaeger's sanitary stockinette combinations in pure animal wool with double thickness over chest and stomach c.1886

Dr. Jaeger's woollen stockingette drawers with double front c.1884

West End. Some of them contained fashionable ladies brought to Jaeger by Oscar Wilde, who was then at the height of his career and who was an ardent friend and disciple of Dr. Jaeger. Another enthusiast was George Bernard Shaw, who is recorded in Frank Harris's biography as having walked up Oxford Street in a Jaeger garment—'a single garment or combination in brown knitted wool, complete from sleeves to ankles, in one piece.' (He did say, much later, 'Jaeger did dreadful things in those days'). This was a literal interpretation of Dr. Jaeger's stipulation to the British Company that clothing should be all-wool, close fitting, made in natural coloured mixed white and brown wools, undyed and unbleached. The original Jaeger undergarments were 100% pure wool, in the stockingette weave approved by the Doctor on health grounds. They had long sleeves, high necks and were double-fronted, for protection. Typical were combinations, for men, women and children, in summer, winter and winter extra thick weights.

Women's clothing, including underclothing, engaged considerable attention from Dr. Jaeger. 'Here', he says, 'habit and prejudice are even more potent than with men.' And he continues: 'I have to declare war against such cherished finery as silk dresses, white petticoats (often starched so as to make them thoroughly impermeable), linen stays, cotton or silk stockings, and white starched dresses.' What he advocates is that 'chemise, stockings, drawers, petticoat and stays should all be made of pure animal wool. These, with a dress of pure woollen stuff, closing well round the throat, and having a double lining at the chest and downwards, should be the winter and summer wear of women.' On the grounds that women wear too many layers of clothes on the lower half of the body, he elsewhere advises combinations instead of chemise and drawers.

As the corset, at that time tight-laced at fashion's behest, was already being attacked on health grounds, it was to be expected that in covering every side of clothing Dr. Jaeger would not pass it over. The Sanitary Woollen Corset appeared in the first 1884 catalogues of Jaeger in London and it continued to appear for many years, right into the present century. Dr. Jaeger himself refers to attacks on the conventional corset of the time by 'some leading authorities on health culture' and comments: 'the fault does not consist wholly in the wearing of a corset, but partly on the material of which it is made. This is usually substantial (possibly even pasted) linen cloth,

and (1) concentrates, in an intensified degree, the disadvantages of
clothing made from vegetable fibre; (2) is, as a rule, laced too tightly,
because the great enervation of the body, caused by wearing this
most unhealthy material, induces a feeling of want of support and
a tendency to unshapely increase of bulk, only to be restrained by
the use of force, under which the internal organs suffer.

'Ladies, however, who have adopted, and especially those who
have grown up under, the Sanitary Corset, need to use no force in
order to preserve the shape; their compact, firm figures will not
require support. They do not therefore lace too tightly, and in the
Sanitary Woollen Corset they have all the advantages of girded loins
without the disadvantages.'

The 1884 'sanitary woollen, spring corsets' were described as
'flexible, elastic, durable, with watch spring steels' and as respond-
ing to every movement of the body. The steels were buttoned in at
the upper end, so that they could be removed for cleaning. The
corsets were made in undyed sheep's wool but also in white and
grey and in camel hair.

Drawers, chemises and petticoats also appear in the 1884
catalogues, and there is a picture of 'sanitary stockinet combinations'.
In 1887 a patent stocking suspender, a belt with the suspenders
attached, was introduced and was one of the earliest examples of
this device to get rid of the constricting garter.

The association of wool with Dr. Jaeger was so strongly established that the compilers of the Oxford Dictionary wanted to include
his name in one of their editions as meaning any pure wool. And at
the time of Queen Victoria's first jubilee Jaeger were doing excellent
business, 'for then her foreign and colonial visitors all drive up to
our shop in royal carriages', according to the recollections of an old
employee.

But even in the underwear world fashion never stays still. The
pure wool corsets remained until the second decade of this century,
following the longer-hipped lines of other corsetry of the time. But
by the 'thirties they were being advertised as 'specially recommended for nurses and invalids'. Children's staybands and corsets
also provided a useful side-line.

But the general styling of women's underwear moved away from
the principles laid down by the good Dr. Jaeger. By 1913 combinations were being made finely ribbed and in white, with short
sleeves and buttoned-up fronts. In 1915 there was 'something quite

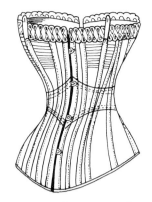

*Dr. Jaeger's pure wool corset
with back lacing and
removable watch-spring steels
c.1886*

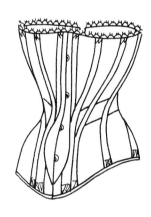

*Another Dr. Jaeger wool
corset with spoon busk c.1886*

new'—a crossover bust bodice in white wool taffeta, and also camisoles. By the 'thirties fashion had won. What would Dr. Jaeger have made of the advertisement of the 'vivacious pantie', showing a girl doing the splits in a brief pantie and a shoulder-strapped vest? In the early 1930's the Company was making 'the world's most serene underneaths', including opera vests and panties, and a little later there were 'spring-knit undies' of pure silk and wool, and silk alone, in fashionable peach, pink and white. By 1933 the corsets were 'specialities for matrons and invalids'.

In the same year the Company state that 'we found after a time that people were inclined to think that health clothing might be ugly. Now Jaeger is known to be the reverse; in fact we are leaders today in smart underwear and outerwear'. In 1933 the Company's house magazine records that 'Miss Gertrude Lawrence bought a large outfit of frocks and beach-wear at Oxford Street to take away on her summer holiday. So did Miss Madeleine Carroll'.

But Dr. Gustav Jaeger can rest in peace. To this day Jaeger still manufacture a substantial amount of underwear in the natural

Jaeger fine ribbed wool combinations 1913

Jaeger combinations in wool crepe, trimmed lace and ribbon and with wide 'French' legs 1917

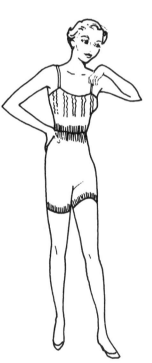

Jaeger vest and pantie in pure wool 1935

Jaeger silk cami-knickers 1938

colour wool he advocated. Both men's and women's underwear is made in the traditional style for export purposes, the largest market being Hong Kong. Sweaters and tweed skirts in wool are also leading export items.

By a curious coincidence only four years after Dr. Jaeger's 'sanitary woollen system' had been launched in Britain in 1884 with immediate success, there came another innovation in underwear fabrics which made a comparable impact upon traditional, centuries-old ideas and upon the undergarments worn by men, women and children.

One great merit of wool, according to Dr. Jaeger, was its porousness. This he denied to cotton and all other materials not of animal origin, but he was soon to be refuted. Late in 1887 the idea of cellular materials was first thought of and in the following year Aertex came into existence. It is still, like Jaeger, a household word and in many ways it has remained even closer to its original conception.

Aertex, like wool, was associated with the health cult of the time. The originator of it was Mr. Lewis Haslam, for many years M.P. for Newport, Mon. The scene of the invention was a sanatorium at Westward Ho, Devon, where, along with Mr. Haslam, were staying two notable members of the medical profession, Sir Benjamin Ward Richardson and Dr. Richard Greene.

Mr. Haslam's starting point was a belief in the value of fresh air. Fresh air should not only be breathed into the lungs but should respirate the skin. It could, he believed, not only have a positive effect on health but also insulate the body against heat and cold. The idea had originally stemmed from a discussion about the warmth which was promoted by wool when it was new and fluffy and therefore contained air, but which ceased to be effective when wool was washed and became felted, as was almost unavoidable in those days.

What was wanted therefore was a material that would continue to hold air through many wearings and washings. Cotton was the answer. Its absorbency would ensure the retention of its stable form. The need was simply to find a weave that provided aerating qualities.

Mr. Haslam carried his two famous medicos with him in this belief and in March 1888 the Aertex Company was set up in a small office in Aldermanbury for the purpose of manufacturing cellular fabrics. Sir Benjamin was chairman and the two other members of the pioneering trio were among the directors. At first only the materials were produced. The new company concentrated its efforts on promoting the idea of the revolutionary fabric with holes in it and on selling Aertex materials to clothing and underclothing manufacturers. The enterprise was a success and the idea of a fabric that would not only be cooler in summer but also warmer in winter caught on so firmly that by November 1889 larger premises were needed. To start with, men's clothing alone was made but in 1891, when Aertex started making up its own garments, the women's underwear market was broached for the first time. This was in another new factory in Gresham Street 'staffed' by one treadle machinist and one finisher. By January 1892 there was a move to Fore Street (where Jaeger also had its premises) and by then there were ten machinists and six other employees.

From this time expansion went on steadily, with a second factory at Swindon in 1901 and consolidation of manufacture at Nottingham some years later. Cellular materials increased in variety and scope. The Victoria and Albert Museum has a pair of white Aertex combinations of the early 1900's. Very utilitarian, they are reinforced with tapes at the darted waist, buttoned all down the front, but trimmed with broderie anglaise at the neck, sleeves and knee-length legs. Today women's Aertex underwear is styled in line with

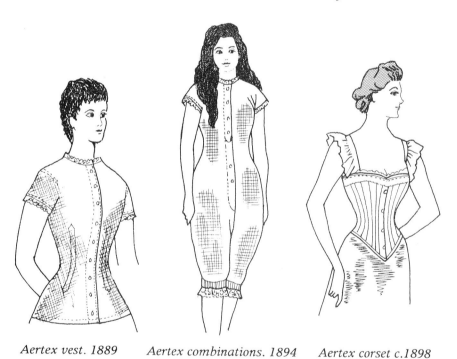

Aertex vest. 1889   *Aertex combinations. 1894*   *Aertex corset c.1898*

fashion and the market for it continues to be an important one, with particular attractions for tropical wear, where the newer synthetics are not satisfactory.

Another underwear fabric that made its mark in the development of materials with health attributes which was to be a main feature of undergarments in the twentieth century was Viyella. Produced by William Hollins & Co. after long experiments in blending wool and cotton in satisfactory proportions and in the best methods of weaving a fabric, Viyella came on the market in a small way in 1891. It was conceived as a fabric for men's shirts and nightshirts, but wider uses soon became evident. In 1894 it became the first fabric to carry a registered trade mark. As the twentieth century brought a powerful swing over from made-to-order underclothing to ready-made garments, Viyella started manufacturing its own garments instead of simply selling the material to manufacturers. This side of the business grew rapidly and extensively from the time of the launching of the first season's range of undergarments in the autumn of 1904. Today Viyella in both woven and knitted under-wear and outer garments is as much a household name as it ever was, and, like Jaeger and Aertex, it has become invested with a fashion quality that has enlivened its character and enlarged its scope. In addition it has maintained its original claim, very noteworthy at the time, that 'Viyella does not shrink', surmounting with vigour a crisis in 1911 when the increasing use of laundries had produced evidence that the claim was vulnerable to new-fangled machine methods.

Aertex vest and knickers. 1938

The biggest influence of all in the transformation of women's underwear in the nineteenth century came, as often happens in history, not by the concentrated conscious efforts of political, social or health reformers but by something else that arrived right out of the blue. It was the bicycle which, as Dr. C. W. Cunnington observes with masterly brevity and completeness, 'converted the lady into a biped and supplied her with a momentum which carried her headlong into the next century'. The original 'penny-farthing' of 1871 had been unmanageable by anyone except a long-legged man, but the safety bicycle, which was introduced in 1885, was widely adopted by both men and women within a few years. The introduction of the pneumatic tyre by Dunlop in 1888 was an additional incentive, and by the early 'nineties women had taken up cycling with fervour. Fashionable ladies even drove to the park

Aertex combinations. 1938

in their carriages complete with bicycle, which was unloaded for a ride when the open spaces were reached. Bloomers and various styles of divided skirts and knickerbockers naturally sprang into fashion and for sport at least dress was becoming 'rational', though slowly.

In the 1890's a suitable cycling costume for women was described as consisting of 'warm combinations, a thick woollen vest or knitted bodice, and a pair of tweed or cloth knickerbockers, with a skirt of waterproofed cloth more close fitting and rather long in front so as to display a not too liberal allowance of ankle.' There were repeated suggestions in magazines of the time that a corset should not be worn for cycling and other active sports. The general advice given was that a flannel bodice should replace the corset, but the 'sanitary woollen corset' of Dr. Jaeger and other woollen corsets were recommended for those who insisted on wearing a corset 'and also, perhaps from habit, could not safely dispense with it.' The substitution of a bodice for the corset is also advised in outfits for various other sports.

Bloomers had an uphill fight to secure recognition, and it was often recommended that they should be worn with a skirt, long or knee-length, so that they wavered between being underwear and outerwear. They were often known as 'rationals' and were criticised on the grounds of inelegance but applauded for their comfort and freedom. By about 1896 they were being worn on their own, without skirts but with hip-length jackets. An alternative, which found considerable favour, was a divided skirt, designed with a pleated frill at the hem, to disguise its separation.

Women engaged in so many sports during the nineteenth century that it is astonishing how slow the contemporary enveloping and restricting fashions were to give way to functional clothes, both under and outer, which allowed for freedom of movement. It was not until the turn of the century that a real advance was made. Up to then women played cricket, hockey, golf and tennis, fished, skated, went shooting, climbed mountains, even went ski-ing either in ankle-length skirts, bloomers, divided skirts or skirts looped up fishwife style on to a deep waistband, over bloomers or knickerbockers. In the 1860's they had even gone climbing in crinolines and in the 1870's they crossed glaciers in ankle-length skirts. The chief concession modern progress made to their apparel was that the wearing of woollen combinations and other woollen under-garments of a more or less functional design, was universally advocated by writers on the subject.

Change was, however, on its way. In no part of fashion is the difference between the Victorian and Edwardian eras more conspicuous than in underwear. The label 'Victorian', which for most of the time since then has been loosely and generally applied to what is old-fashioned, hidebound and fusty, is in some ways more fully justified in underwear than in many other respects. It applied to the bulk, the rigidity and the multiplication of garments. But it was, as already stated, Victorian England that introduced lace trimming and embroidery to underwear in general and the first silk underwear was made in the 1880's.

What mainly happened was that the Edwardian mood, in fact, anticipated history and established itself by the 'gay 'nineties', while the future King Edward VII was still Prince of Wales. But it produced a revolutionary change. With the old Queen living more or less in retirement, society was dominated by the Prince and the fashionable way of life that prevailed in his circles was lavish, assertive, luxurious and given to embracing all the pleasures of life on a sumptuous scale. Vast country houses, opulently run by hordes of servants, enormous banquets where course followed course, luxurious entertaining and pervasive luxury formed the framework of society and it naturally affected fashion. The moral earnestness reflected throughout later Victorian life had not been destroyed, but so far as fashion was concerned it had at least gone underground. Fashion for less exalted people took its keynote, as in the past, from what the wealthy favoured.

In underwear there was, however, one curious amalgam of the new luxury look with the increasing concern with health and fitness. A notable innovation in corsetry design was the 'health' corset, pioneered by Dr. Jaeger, as already described. A great number of other designs with similar aims came on the market at the turn of the century.

Worth, who established the first of the Paris couture houses and whose clients were headed by the elegant Empress Eugénie, was concerned in the movement to introduce a straight-busked corset and do away with the figure distortion of the then existent style with waist indentation. But the forces which later brought the idea into being were Dr. Franz Glénard and Mme Gaches-Sarraute, whose name is closely associated with the innovation. A corsetière who

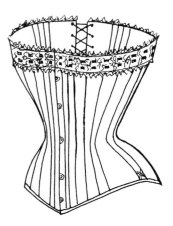

Straight busk in a pale grey cotton corset with back lacing c. 1905

had studied medicine, she set out to design corsets that would aid health instead of harming or endangering it. She realised the importance of leaving the thorax free yet of supporting the abdomen. She was responsible for the actual introduction of the straight-fronted busk, aimed at supporting and raising the abdomen instead of compressing it and forcing it downwards. By getting rid of the constricting inward curve at the waist, customary in all previous corsets, Madame Gaches-Sarraute aimed at removing pressure on the diaphragm and abdomen and therefore upon vital female organs. Women would at last have room to move and breathe freely and there would be no more harmful compression round and below the waist.

A similar innovation was Carlson's Patent Binder Corset, which was advertised with an impressive list of claims: 'This invention has been submitted by the inventors to the highest medical authorities, both in England and in France, and they unanimously declare that when generally known it will be universally adopted BY ALL CLASSES and entirely supersede the clumsy, heavy corset of the present time. Compression can be regulated to one-sixteenth of an inch, and a perfect figure can be secured while at the same time it materially assists, WITHOUT UNDUE PRESSURE, to obviate the tendency to *embonpoint'*.

Had the purposes of the 'health' corset been achieved it would have been a substantial move towards the production of a corset that would reinforce the natural pull of the muscles between waist and hips and thereby become a valuable health agent. But unfortunately the craze for the small waist persisted. The new health corset was laced up as tightly as its unhealthy forbears, and as a result a new distortion of the figure was created. This was the famous 'S' curve. It was brought about by the fact that if the corset was laced too tightly the new straight busk would push the bust prominently forward and throw the hips back to an extreme degree of physical distortion.

This shape, with lavish bust and impressive hips, conformed to the current ideal of beauty. For the last time between then and now the mature, voluptuous figure with ample curves both at bosom and hips was the fashionable aim. It remained so during the first years of the present century: it accorded well with the Edwardian way of life.

Curves on the bosom were even more important than on the hips,

1903–4 Gibson Girl 'S' shaped corset

and lack of them was more frequent. The new straight corset could not, like the earlier styles, come high up in front and support or even push up the bust. Its straight line would have made this construction torture, so it left the bust largely unsupported. For this reason and because busts were fashionable, there was an increase in the wearing of various styles of bust bodice and of numerous kinds of bust improvers, from pads and other artificial shape-makers to camisoles with stiffly starched tiers of frills in front to produce an impressive frontage. Edwardian bosoms were worn low, and they overhung the waist, in contrast to the fashions of the mid-twentieth century, which went to the other extreme of 'uplift', and there was as yet no hint at all of cleavage or even of any suggestion of division between the breasts. The female bosom was emphatically bow-fronted.

The epitome of the new figure of fashion was the famous 'Gibson Girl', the exaggerated 'S' shaped-figure immortalised in the drawings of Charles Dana Gibson, the American artist, in the early years of this century and embodied on the stage by Miss Camille Clifford. The cult reached its peak about 1905.

At the same time that the feminine figure was being thus changed by the corset, other underwear was not standing still. The discreet linens, lawns and cottons of Victorian underwear, gave place, fashion-wise, to the finest of silks and to undergarments that were light and airy to a degree quite new in the whole history of fashion. A pair of combinations of the year 1905, now in the Victoria and Albert Museum Collection, is of the softest and lightest black silk, trimmed with a profusion of very fine écru lace which is slotted through with pink baby ribbon. The legs, still inordinately long and reaching well below any normal knee level, are edged with immense frills of deeply pointed lace. So great is the visible change that it is surprising to find that the garment retains the old open style. The legs are almost in two separate pieces, being joined to the top half only at the back of the waist with fine gatherings. There is buttoning all down the front, to a similar opening there from the top of the legs to well down them.

To the same year, 1905, belongs a pair of black silk knickers (as drawers were now being described) of equal fineness. They carry the fashionable label of Woollands, then located at 2 Lowndes Terrace, S.W.1. and not in the later Knightsbridge site where the famous fashion store stood until it closed in 1967. These knickers

'Gibson Girl' 'S' shape in white cotton lace and ribbon-trimmed camisole and petticoat c.1903–5

Matching French knickers in black silk, trimmed with lace and ruching c.1905

Fine black silk combinations trimmed with lace and slotted pink ribbon c.1905

too consist of two almost separate very long leg pieces, and again the only join is at the back of the waist. The fronts are entirely separate, crossing over with fastenings when the garment is put on. There are rows of tiny tucks at the back waistline, and again a profuse amount of lace insertion and frilling edges the wide legs.

Looking at these examples of fashionable underwear one understands the insistence of the wearers on describing the garments as 'lingerie' for the first time. Nothing comparable had ever before been worn. 'Edwardian underclothes', say the Cunningtons, 'developed a degree of eroticism never previously attempted . . . women had learned much, since the 1870's, of the art of suggestion . . . they invented a silhouette of fictitious curves, massive above, with rivulets of lacy embroidery trickling over the surface down to a whirlpool of froth at the foot.'

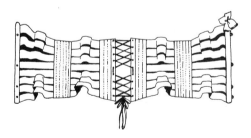

1900 pink satin ribbon corset, with back lacing and front busk

It is not surprising that petticoats were advertised at as much as fifty guineas and were made of silk, satin, moiré and various other luxury fabrics. One example, showing how opulence could be secured at a bargain price too, is accorded a large illustration in a Debenham & Freebody sale catalogue of the early 1900's. It is part of a 'special offer of 1000 silk moirette underskirts, extra rich quality, perfectly fresh, cut in the newest style, extra full, in spots, stripes and chine effects. All colours, extra large and full.' In the picture the petticoat streams out all round with a foaming sea of frilling, ankle-length in front but sweeping the floor at the back, in the prevailing style of fashions of the time. No wonder contemporary fashion journals write of underwear in elaborately emotional and ecstatic terms and always with a degree of solemnity which has never before or afterwards been accorded to the subject. Snobbery was supreme in underwear: when plebeian pink flannelette combinations are mentioned in a ladies' magazine it is stressed that 'we must not call these lingerie.'

It is curious that, parallel to this frou-frou and seductiveness in underwear, there was proceeding the increasing participation of women in sport and other physical activities, for which underwear was of a sober, practical and even formidable kind that ran to the opposite extreme of the fashionable 'frillies'.

How remote from traditional femininity sportswear could be is shown by a golfing costume of 1905, also at the Victoria and Albert Museum. It is made of brown and black striped tweed of a weight we would expect to be used for a man's winter overcoat. The Norfolk style jacket is strapped down the sides with cross-cut bands of material. It is belted, buttoned and has storm collar and cuffs of stout beige leather. The voluminous ankle-length skirt is also banded at the hem with an extra strip of material. To complete the outfit there is a hat—or rather an outsize version of a man's cap, as wide as a large dinner plate, with a peak in front. The ensemble must have constituted a heavy handicap for even the most adept early lady golfer and in the spirit of the time it would have had underneath it underwear of the intimidatingly 'practical' type adopted by the earlier and contemporary cycling woman and by the new legion of country walkers.

Examples of such practical undergarments exist alongside the beguiling 'frillies'. There is, for example, in the Victoria and Albert Museum Collection a very worthy pair of long yellow flannel

1902 purple and black striped silk petticoat; gathered frills with bands of velvet ribbon and black lace edging

drawers belonging to 1909, with a deep cotton waistband, cotton buttons and the usual centre front and back opening, extending to the waistband. They are very prosaic indeed. The knee-band is also buttoned, and to judge by their size they must have extended almost to the calves of E. Roote, whose name-tab they carry.

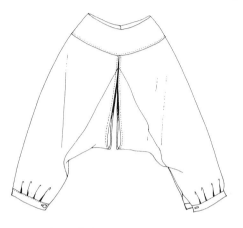

Flannel drawers with cotton bands at waist and legs. Buttoned at back c.1909

7 | *Following a Straight Line: 1905–1927*

Corset in satin broché with low bust, deep hips and two pairs suspenders, worn with nainsook chemise c.1910

Similar corset in strong batiste c.1910

Fashion never stays still, and the days of the mature full-blown beauty in her flowing skirts and frothing, befrilled and copiously shaped underwear were almost over. By 1907 the curvacious 'S' figure was on its way out, and fashion was favouring a slim, willowy shape and a close-fitting Empire line in clothes, with rather high waists and ever-narrowing skirts.

This demanded underwear that was not only fine but also clinging. Out went those voluminous, romantic petticoats. The corset became steadily longer below the waist and in 1908 it was described in a fashion journal as being 'cut so deep that to sit down would appear an impossible feat.' This very long corset persisted for a number of years, while the narrow skirt remained in fashion, and it was, of course, boned, laced up the back and fastened in front with the busk fastening. It had heavy suspenders, which fastened on to the stockings round about the knee.

At the same time the bust bodice continued to increase in popularity, although in the early years of this century there were no outstanding changes in its construction. The whalebone front,

Boned bust bodice in white cotton c.1913

with the bow-windowed effect, continued to be accepted, and the device of fronts formed of tiers of starched frills was also still favoured by those whose natural curves were insufficient for the ample bustline which fashion favoured even when skirts were narrow.

The word 'brassière' is recorded by the Oxford Dictionary as having been introduced in 1912. It was used prior to that date in America, where in 1907 an illustration in *Vogue* was captioned 'the brassière'. Why this word brassière was adopted is something of a mystery. Although French, it is obsolete there in the meaning of a bodice, and neither was nor is used in France in the sense given it to replace the earlier 'bust bodice'. In French a brassière is usually an infant's under-bodice. Larousse's famous dictionary cites various other meanings, including a harness and, in the plural, leading strings or the shoulder straps of a rucksack, but not our 'brassière'. In France this garment is known as a *soutien-gorge*. The origin of our word would seem to lie with someone with an imperfect knowledge of French: dare we blame America for inventing the name? The now prevalent diminutive, 'bra', does not appear to have been used before about 1937.

In the pre-war years petticoats, unlike brassières, changed in style completely, and although still made of fine silk for the fashion trade, they were slim, with no more of the gathered flounces that a few years before had required five or six yards of broderie anglaise, lace or frilling. Sometimes petticoats were even dispensed with, to ensure an even slimmer figure, and at the same time the directoire and other closed styles of knickers began to be more generally worn. This, like the other changes in underwear, was a move towards modern thinking on the subject, but for a number of years both open and closed styles of knickers co-existed. It was not till after the First World War that the latter gained its dominance. It was foreshadowed, however, well before the War in a garment called a 'skirt knicker' or 'divided skirt', which was first worn round about 1906–8, when the slimmer Empire line was being introduced into fashion. It had wide skirt legs, like the open-style knickers and combinations, currently worn, and its design makes it the precursor both of the post-1914 war French knickers and of cami-knickers. Descriptions exist of how the skirt was buttoned between the legs, to make it serve as both knickers and petticoat, and it was still a familiar and fashionable garment in the nineteen-twenties.

Narrow satin under-skirt with pleated hem. 1910

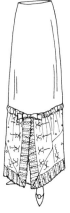

Slim evening under-skirt in Jap silk with lace flounce. 1910

During these pre-war years underwear was continuing to become more modern in materials and conception, though many designs still remained traditional. Thus a pair of 1913 combinations, now in the Victoria and Albert Museum Collection, is made of gossamer-fine white lawn, trimmed with a mass of very delicate lace at bust and legs. There are pink satin ribbon shoulder straps, foreshadowing a future almost universal feature of underwear, and pink satin ribbon is slotted round the bust and waist. There is much elaboration of lace at the legs, the outside edges of which are slightly cut up to allow further lace trimming. But this garment is still open between the legs both back and front, the join occurring only at the waist and knees. A pair of knickers, dated 1912, has the same characteristics of being made of material fine enough in texture to please the most modern taste, lavishly frilled with lace, plus lace insertion, tucks and embroidery. They are darted on to a narrow waistband and are buttoned down the sides, but they too remain open nearly to the waist.

Cambric combination-petticoat with tucks, lace insertion, embroidery and slotted ribbon c.1910

Nainsook camisole and knickers, tucked and trimmed with lace c. 1910
(right) Lace and ribbon-trimmed combined camisole and knickers 1910

Lawn combinations with ribbon drawstrings and lace trimming c.1913

Fine white lawn open knickers with embroidered net and lace insertion, drawstring at back c.1912

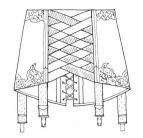

Lace-trimmed corset with front section of criss-cross satin ribbon. c.1914

This slimming-down of underwear, without any basic new thinking about its design, was consistent with the rather gradual change in outer fashions once the 'S' shape had been discarded. The most significant influence exerted by the slimmer skirts, which culminated in 1911 in a 'hobble' skirt so tight that walking could be difficult, was that tight-lacing was out. The higher Empire waistline and the slim skirt meant that there was no longer any tightly defined waistline. Hips had to be slim, so a straight line was the feature of the corset. Tight-lacing died—and has never since then been revived.

Women of 1914 felt that they were well and truly emancipated. An advertisement in the *Sketch* of April 12, 1914 proclaims: 'The revolution in woman's dress demands also a revolution in corsetting her. Freedom is the dominant note in all that relates to modern woman, and it is this freedom which Marshall & Snelgrove have so successfully achieved in their new style of corsetting, without any loss of graceful symmetry.'

Another call to freedom rang out in America in 1913 when Mary Phelps Jacob (later better known as Caresse Crosby) invented a new kind of brassière that was soft, short and so designed that it gave clear natural separation between the breasts. Then a fashionable New York débutante, she was in revolt against the whalebone bodices and corsets of the time and she contrived her bra with the help of her French maid, using two handkerchiefs and baby ribbon. Later she was persuaded to make copies of it for friends and then she planned to exploit it. She called it the Backless Bra and in November 1914 she was granted a patent for it and planned to market it, but was unsuccessful in doing so. She lost interest, but later, after her marriage to the first of her three millionaire husbands, she sold the patent to Warner Bros. Subsequently in her book *The Passionate Years* she claims of 'the brassière' that 'I did invent it.' In fact she invented one design, but the garment had been in existence by name for at least six years and in a great variety of shapes since the last decade of the nineteenth century. It had, however, always been long, coming over the corset, and it was boned and rigid. She introduced the modern concept of a brief style which was free of bones and which left the midriff free. In that respect her design was revolutionary and pioneered future trends that would begin to show themselves in the 1920's. She lived to see innumerable developments in the bra, and died early in 1970.

Caresse Crosby's 1914 brassière

The chief fashion innovation of the immediate pre-wars years was the tunic—a fuller skirt over the 'hobble'—and its main significance is that when the demands of war caught up with women, the 'hobble' was discarded and the remaining tunic, slightly lengthened, paved the way to above-ankle fashions for the first time in fashion history.

It is still usual to regard the 1914–1918 war as a great and complete line of demarcation between old and new in the entire structure of life—economic, political, social and so on. The bland, mellow sunlight of the Edwardian age and all its elaborate conventions and class distinctions ended. 'The lights are going out all over Europe'. A new and different world was to emerge when the war was over.

While the effects of this cataclysm were immense, great forces of social change in big things and small had been building up for many years before 1914 and they proceeded after 1918 on a course that had not been entirely conditioned or reshaped by the war, but in some respects was merely halted by it.

To fashion the war did not at first bring any significant change, because for the first year at least civilian life as a whole was not basically greatly affected. Women's organisations, despite their immediate offers of help, were pushed aside. Then, in 1915, the need for them was realised and in Britain the Women's Service Bureau recruited one and a half million women for civilian jobs, where they replaced men. In addition to pouring into munition and other factories women became civil servants (162,000 of them went into the new ministries set up in Whitehall), house painters, electricians, van drivers, bus conductors, porters and 'signalmen' on the railways. In 1917 they were introduced into the Police force, and early in that year the first regular women's service corps, the Women's Army Auxiliary Corps, was formed, to be quickly followed by the Women's Royal Naval Service and the Women's Royal Air Force Service. In these and supplementary services 150,000 women were enrolled.

The fashions, both outer and under, of the latter years of the war seem in photographs to be largely a continuation of the rather fussy and much-trimmed pre-war trends, with skirts still near the ankles. This was to be expected because the effect of the war on fashion was to a large extent to bring it to a standstill, as the later 1939–45 war was also to do. The reasons were the same and quite obvious—a

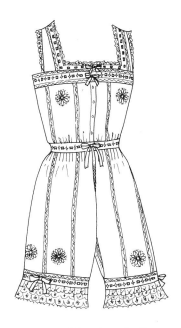

1916 combinations in finest cotton trimmed with ribbon-slotted lace insertion and frills

1916 *matching chemise*

complete change in the activities of women, which meant lack of time and inclination for fashion, together with shortages of materials and labour and the pressure of tragedies and anxieties which put the trivialities of life out of mind. In a world of food queues, scarcities of everyday needs and, for most families, the overhanging dread of those endless casualty lists, fashion had little place, even for women not actively involved in war work.

The main footnote to fashion history contributed by the 1914–18 war was a fashion that never was. This was an attempt in 1918 to introduce into Britain a National Standard Dress for women—a garment without hooks or eyes or metal buckles, which was designed to be an 'outdoor gown, house gown, rest gown, tea gown, dinner gown, evening dress and nightgown'. The mind boggles. It was the first and last attempt of the kind.

There was, however, some progress made on the wearing of brassières during the war. Whether this was partly due to the realisation that the support of this garment contributes both to health and comfort (as was to be promulgated later), it is difficult to say. Probably at that time brassière designing had not got far in this direction. The main need for a brassière was that the softer fashion lines of the immediate pre-war years were maintained in clothing. In 1915 it was said that 'a pretty bust bodice or a brassière counts quite as much an essential as a corset'. 'Gowns of utmost softness and semi-transparency have made a bust support essential', advises a fashion magazine in 1916. Evening dresses were of this type and so was the less formal and increasingly popular house dress, precursor of the later cocktail dress. In what seems a parody of a wartime rallying, all-together call, another fashion publication, *The Lady*, in the same year declares of brassières: 'The French and American women all wear them and so must we'. Friends and allies, stand together!

The real effect of the 1914–18 war upon fashion lay, however, far below the surface of what was being worn or not worn during those years. It sprang from the new, changed outlook of women, which was reflected strongly in post-war clothes.

During the war years for the first time in modern history women in the mass were experiencing independence. They were being well paid. They were being given responsibility and were proving themselves worthy of it. The immediate result in Britain was the giving of the vote to all women over thirty in the Representation of the

People Act which, after a long course of several months in both Houses of Parliament, finally received the Royal Assent on 6th February 1918. In 1928 the franchise was extended to women on the same terms as men, at the age of twenty-one, and the much talked of (but inaccurate) 'Flapper Vote' came into existence.

The effect of this change of status was, naturally, not universally apparent at once, nor did it rapidly affect what all women wore. Some immediate post-war underwear seems to show little sign of this political revolution. Cami-knickers of 1920 at the Victoria and Albert Museum, which present closed and open styles simultaneously, continue in the pre-war tradition of fussy prettiness. An English pair of cami-knickers (the name had become usual about 1916) are richly decorated with lace, with ribbon shoulder straps but are open from the waist. Of the same year is a French pair, again with lots of lace, both as edging and as inserts, fine pleats, pink satin shoulder straps—but these are in the closed style, with a very big gusset. Closed directoire knickers, dated 1919, are in the same collection. They are of fine silk in violet and black stripes, with elastic at the waist and at the legs, which are finished with a frill and a bow at the outside. What mainly dates them is that, like all underwear of the time, they are so astonishingly big.

Pale pink silk combinations with embroidered net bodice and frills c.1920

Closed cami-knickers in cream silk with fine pleating and wide bands of lace insertion c. 1920

That, however, was not to continue for much longer. In 1919 there started a figure change which was to have not only speedy but also very long-lasting effects upon underwear, and was to swing it into a course of simplification which, generally speaking, it has pursued ever since. For the first time there was a move to flatten the bosom, to narrow the hips and to bypass the waist. The 'boyish' figure was the aim.

The thinking behind this 'flat' fashion was two-fold. Firstly, in the first flush of emancipation and the 'equality' signified by the vote and the increasing acceptance of the working girl and the career woman, it was natural, if impulsive and rather unconsidered, for women to rush to demonstrate their equality by suppressing physical differences. They wore tailor-made costumes, cut their hair short and flattened their busts just as they carried their own latch-keys and lived their own lives in economic independence. Secondly, the new fashion was a young trend fostered by the young women who, glorying in their careers and possessed of substantial spending power, became a valuable part of the fashion market and one which the trade began to cater for to a new extent. It has continued to do so, increasingly, ever since.

The immediate result was that fashion, which for hundreds of years had lived by exaggerating in turn the main physical feminine characteristics, now set about eliminating these features. The ideal figure was a straight line. The hem remained near ankle-length until 1925, when it rose up and remained near the knee until 1930, but the 'waistline' was during this whole period almost non-existent, being located round the hips. So far as the flat look was concerned, the brassière assumed a form as unlike the Edwardian and pre-war bust bodice as could be imagined. It became a flattener pure and simple. An essential part of the straight boyish look, it was a single, slightly side-darted but otherwise straight, tight band, usually of strong cotton or firm broché and fastened down one side. It ran round the body to the waist, with shoulder straps to keep it in place. Its aim was to combine with a dead-straight corset to distribute flesh evenly from chest to abdomen, regardless of natural contours and anatomy.

Nearly every corset manufacturer now came into the brassière market. One famous style was presented in 1922 with the claim that it was the only one to 'give the wearer a perfectly flat form from the shoulder to hem . . . and does not push up the bust.' Many of

Flat look lace brassière with back fastening c. 1925

these brassières still exist in the collections maintained by certain corset companies, notably Symingtons of Market Harborough. In materials like heavy broché, usually pink, they were made with little change of style for many years. Some had side fastenings and others had all-elastic backs and no fastening; therefore they must have passed over the head.

What effect had this flat figure on the corset? For those whose natural curves had to be suppressed, corsets were very necessary. Various wrap-round styles, with front busks, were worn, usually low on the hips and rising only slightly above the waist. Some of these, made of rigid materials and with a lot of bones and back-lacing, persisted for nearly half a century as a profitable, if decreasing, section of the corset trade. Older women, who had been used to this kind of 'armour', did not want to give it up and it continued to be made during their lifetime. It has barely died out today.

Elastic was, however, beginning to be used to an appreciable extent in corsetry and shop catalogues of the time refer to 'corsets of woven porous elastic' (1923) and to wrap-round rubber corsets (1925). It was obvious that the new flat figure, designed mainly for youth, would open the way to the wearing of much lighter and less constricting corsets than had been usual and also to the adoption of lightweight suspender belts, worn only to keep up the stockings. A great variety of such corsets and belts can be seen in costume collections and store catalogues and, though some of them seem strange, a considerable number are recognisably the forerunners of what has been worn in recent years, and still is.

As the aim of the corset and brassière now was to provide an unbroken flat line down the whole torso, it was a logical conclusion that a one-piece garment would soon be evolved with this in view. What was at first known as the corsolette appeared in America in 1919 and in Britain a year or two later. 'After years of separation', stated a U.S. corset trade publication's retrospective survey, 'with high and low-bust corsets, the fully confining brassière and the corset became integrated in one completely supporting garment. It was laced, boned and gusseted within an inch of the wearer's life, but it was the first modern foundation.' There were also long brassières, with suspenders attached, for flapper trend-setters who wanted to throw away their corsets along with their inherited inhibitions.

Woven corset and 'flattener' bra c.1923

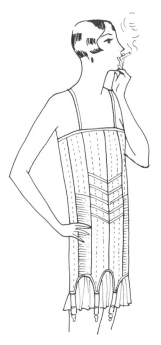

Corselette in mercerised cotton with side panels of knitted elastic c.1925

Broché corselette with elastic side panels. 1928

The new tubular line of fashion offered no compromise with underwear that had always been identified with the exploitation of feminine curves. As a result the 'twenties was a period of continual change. Underwear, in addition to becoming much less bulky and complicated, was peeled down and far fewer garments were worn. The chemise was narrow and brief, and was an alternative to the newer vest, which was soon to oust it completely—and be in its turn relegated to winter only. Knickers became shorter and less full. The waist petticoat, with all its pomposity and frilling, was transformed and finally disappeared almost entirely, and the Princess petticoat, renamed the Princess slip and then simply the slip, took over. It too became much simpler—usually a straight length of material with ribbon shoulder straps.

A feature of the 'twenties was the number of combined garments introduced. Already there was the cami-knicker, introduced during the war, about 1916, but enjoying its heyday in the 'twenties and 'thirties. More ephemeral, but newsworthy at the time, were the various complicated multiple garments. In 1923, when skirts were still ankle-length and the silhouette was soft, clinging and rather drooping, Debenham & Freebody disclosed 'the secret of slenderness' in a group of composite undergarments that offered various different permutations of what would normally be several separate items. Pride of place went to the 'Corslo' silhouette, 'bust bodice, hip belt, jupon and pantaloon combined, top part of best quality double satin, buttoned at the back, and boned with two steels in front to support the figure, the two pairs of suspenders attached to the garment are hidden by the knickers; the skirt and knickers of heavy laundry pleated Crepe de Chine. Measurements required when ordering: bust, waist and hips.'

The illustration shows a long flat bra, with shoulder straps, a belt and an accordion pleated ankle-length petticoat. A smaller drawing reveals how the stockings were attached by concealed suspenders under concealed knickers. It was the start of co-ordinates.

There was also the new 'Corslo-Pantaloon'. When you put it on 'you have thus instantly put on the equivalent of chemise, knickers, corset and camisole and have secured the naturally supple and straight slender figure effect which is absolutely demanded by the new fashion'. It was made in cotton tricot, crepe de Chine, ajoure and silk tricot, at various prices.

In addition, the new 'Corslo' was a recognisable corselette, but soft and easy to wear, in contrast to the original grim American version of 1919. It is advocated as a garment suitable for wear with 'the most fashionable day and evening gowns and dance dresses, while, as absolute freedom for every movement is essential to the success and enjoyment of tennis and golf, etc., it is a necessity and boon to the sportswoman'.

Very high prices, in comparison to those of today, are a feature of the good quality underwear of the years between the wars. Matching sets of nightdress and underwear are usual, and some reason for their costliness may be that good quality garments were still all hand-made. It is surprising and rather daunting to recall that this hand workmanship was a general feature of such underwear not only then but also up to the 1939–45 war. Notable too is the range of colours offered in the 'twenties. It is far wider than would normally be obtainable today and comprises, in one typical example, pink, sky, mauve, yellow, peach, coral, ivory, champagne, saxe, vieux rose, cyclamen, apple green, jade and black.

Other similar underwear is made in pure silk milanese, also at high prices and in a choice of from six to ten colours. Combinations are made in lace wool, as are chemises and knickers. Cashmere and silk combinations were also worn by the fashionable woman of this time and were made in pink and white, but the chemises and knickers also came in sky, mauve and lemon.

Within a year or two curves began to creep back into fashion and though in 1925 'waists' were still round the hipline, there was a suggestion of bust and hips. Skirts were also rising and in 1925 were half-way between ankle and knee. A brassière of this date has an adjustable centre front strap which breaks the flat bandeau front and suggests the coming introduction of bust cups because for the first time it separates the two breasts. An unusual garment of this time, illustrated in store catalogues, looks like an early corselette but is described as 'for use as a brassière and corset cover to disguise the line of the corset and give a perfectly smooth effect. It can also be used for bathing'—presumably under the swim-suit. It comes in white or black mesh materials in two qualities and a large range of sizes. It seems to have been a success, because it appears again in 1927 and 1928, by which time it is made in artificial silk—a new arrival.

Catalogues also show a 'combined bust bodice and hip confiner', with a lace top and the promise of firm control over the hips. It is

New style brassière and corset cover in mesh material. 1925

Combined bust bodice and hip confiner in broché with lace top. 1925

*Topless corset with back
lacing, worn with milanese
silk vest. 1925*

made in two qualities of pink broché with lace top, and also in black. A hip girdle has elastic side sections and 'good diaphragm control'. It is a low corset, starting at the waist, straight and firm-looking, and made in various styles. Very similar is a well-designed 'topless corset' (a prophecy of the 'sixties and Rudi Gernreich) in broché, but something with a difference is a 'rubber reducing girdle with front or back lacing and lightly boned'. In pink covered rubber, it is made for tall or short figures.

Other lingerie of 1925, recorded in catalogues, consists mainly of matching sets of nightdress, chemise and knickers in satin or crepe de Chine, but there are now more cami-knickers than in 1923. They include 'new shape step-in' cami-knickers and two other pretty designs, described as 'exact copy of French model'. Princess petticoats hang straight from shoulder straps and have, naturally, become shorter.

There are other garments in fine lawn, including hand-made linen lawn cami-knickers and an embroidered pair, with fine pleated side

*Silk milanese vest with skirt
knicker to match. 1925*

*Step-in cami-knicker in
crepe de Chine. 1925*

*Cami-knickers trimmed
lace. 1925*

*Crepe de Chine cami-knickers
with elastic at knee and lace
trimming. 1927*

panels, in French lawn—again hand-made. Milanese silk is another favourite fabric for vests and matching 'skirt knickers'. Waist petticoats, slim and narrow, are numerous and include a sports petticoat in crepe de Chine, with slits at the sides; one in pleated shantung, another in 'super milanese'; a yoked one in printed crepe de Chine and a 'dainty' one in 'the best quality crepe de Chine, exquisitely hand-embroidered in Richelieu work'—which can be made to order in three days in any colour desired!

Kestos brassière. 1927

The hint of curves was, however, gaining strength. In 1926 it is stated that 'the bust was emphasised and the waistline indicated'. Women were becoming women again. In 1926–7 came the real start of the shaped bust cup that was to be the main justification of the existence of the brassière in succeeding years. Mrs. Rosalind Klin, Polish-born director of the Kestos company, was unable to find a brassière that suited her taste and her interpretation of fashion's trends. She therefore started experimenting and, oddly enough, began exactly as did Caresse Crosby in 1913, with two handkerchiefs. She folded these crosswise and joined them into one piece with an overlap in front. Shoulder straps were sewn on to the top point at each side of the bust and on to the end of the 'hypotenuse' of her two triangles. Elastic was attached there, and, after being crossed at the back, was buttoned to the brassière under each 'cup', which was darted under the bust to give it more shape. This style became almost the synonym for the brassière for many years. You didn't buy a brassière, you bought a 'Kestos'. Other variations followed, and the shape is very similar to that of the 'no-bra' of 1965 and of many of the very natural-shaped bras of 1969 and 1970.

Once shaping and separation had been achieved, further developments in the brassière were to be expected. Deeper bust cups were achieved in 1928 by a disc-like construction of the two sides. Circular stitching, so popular in the 1950's, was also first introduced as a way of giving a rounded shape about 1928.

The new idea of the brassière as a controlling garment, and not a flattener (as in the early 1920's) or a bust-maker (as in the later nineteenth and early twentieth centuries) caught on quickly. In 1927 advertisements showed an 'uplift bodice in good quality silk tricot'. It was a bandeau bra with two rounded cups. Another style was 'a one-piece garment of elastic and tricot, designed for a figure requiring an elastic hip belt, with some bust control above waist. Made in cotton or silk elastic'. 'Control' is mentioned in descriptions of all

Short Princess petticoat in crepe de Chine with lace flounce. 1927

Knickers in crepe de Chine with all-over lace flounces and matching chemise; held are satin knickers finished at knees with 3 rows elastic. 1927

the other corsets featured in that year, except for a hookside belt for dance or sports wear, in 'pink material'.

Princess petticoats, at fashion's dictate, were now knee-length, like outer fashions, and were almost indistinguishable from cami-knickers. Another of the combined garments favoured at this time was a petticoat with directoire knickers attached, made in crepe de Chine, trimmed with écru lace. There were also cami-shorts—the shorts buttoning up the sides but otherwise 'little boy' style. Some designs were very fanciful. Knickers had rows upon rows of narrow lace on the legs; they were covered entirely with lace flouncing; they had deep fitted bands at the knee. And, like the other under-wear, they were 'in all colours'.

An innovation, which was to herald a revolution in underwear fabrics, was mentioned quite unobtrusively in a 1927 catalogue. It appeared in the description of a 'locknit artificial silk unladderable Princess, excellent for wear', made in the usual wealth of colours. Cami-knickers in artificial silk milanese were another item, and there were vests, knickers and a 'cami-petticoat' in the same material.

The following year, 1928 saw little change in catalogued offerings of fashion, but cami-breeches, which look exactly like camibockers, are there. An unexpected item is a lace camisole 'suitable for evening wear'. This was the last stand of this garment, rarely worn by 1929. Locknit artificial silk, 'unladderable', again appears as a popular underwear fabric.

Corsetry showed some innovations. There was a deep brassière in artificial silk, with 'firm control across the diaphragm' and, as was usual then, long suspenders to anchor it to the stockings. A very straight-line 'one-piece garment'—a corselette—in white broché was described as 'suitable for many types of figure'. An elastic pull-on belt in pink cotton elastic was a newcomer, heralding the great progress being made at this time in the manufacture of elastic for corsetry. There was also an uplift bodice, in net, a brief brassière with two distinct cups and a separating section in the front, meant for a small or medium figure and made in sizes 30–34. What we would call a long brassière was also described as a bodice 'to cover the top of a low corset'.

The nineteen-twenties, in addition to paring down feminine curves and establishing a 'girlish' style of dress, also modified many of the words hitherto used to describe underwear. Cami-knickers

Deep brassière with artificial silk bust section and firm control across diaphragm. 1928

Corselette in broché with elastic gussets. 1928

Uplift brassière in net for slight figures, worn with boneless girdle with elastic side panels. 1928

was, of course, from about 1916 used to describe a new garment, but underwear, from the elegant late Victorian and Edwardian description of 'lingerie', became collectively 'undies'. Petticoats were called colloquially 'petties' before they became 'slips'. Knickers were 'knicks', then in the 'thirties, pants and panties and finally, but not till the 'fifties, became 'briefs'. Combinations, on their way out, became 'combs' and the brassière after being called a 'B.B.', became the 'bra' about 1937.

8 | *Back to Nature : 1927 – 1939*

By the late 1920's the centuries-long artificial shape-making of women's figures had become a thing of the past and since then, for more than forty years, it has remained so, with one or two minor exceptions. These, to be dealt with in due course, were mainly the built-up square shoulders of the years before, during and after the Second World War, and the exaggerated bosoms of the mid-fifties. Both of these differed from previous extravagances of fashion history in that they were entirely surface effects. The body beneath them remained natural and free of constriction or distortion, as it was before and after these artificial excrescences.

Corsetry, the obvious function of which is to improve on nature, for aesthetic or erotic reasons, was by this time doing so, as it still does, by means of a control and a moulding of the figure which respected nature. Increasingly, this purpose has been based upon understanding by corset companies and their designers of the anatomical structure of the body; of its bones, muscles and tissues and of the means by which foundation garments can not only follow nature but lend a helping hand when nature fails. Inevitably it must often do so, through imperfections in physique, weak muscles, excessive or insufficient weight and, despite all the care in the world, the inevitable ageing and therefore deterioration of the body.

This function of corsetry was expressed quite early in the 'health corset' of 1911, which was a narrow and, by the standards of that time, a very unrestricting garment. But the pioneer work in this direction had started nearly fifty years before, although with little practical effect at that time on the general lines of corsetry, which were to advance hand in hand with the unnatural extremes and figure distortions of Victorian and even Edwardian fashion.

In 1867 a doctor proposed that the corset should be discarded and the crinoline suspended from the shoulders by braces so that constriction and weight could be taken away from the waist. A camisole, stiffened if need be, was also suggested as an alternative to the corset, with drawers and petticoats buttoned on to it. As this kind of underwear was inconceivable under the fashionable crinoline and, later, the bustle and long, tight bodice, a kind of anticipation of the 'sack' of the 1950's had to be specified as outerwear. Needless to say, the fashion-reform failed.

The first practical efforts towards liberating women's figures began when two American doctor brothers, Drs. Lucien G. Warner and I. de Ver Warner, after serving in the Civil War, returned to New York to write books on women's diseases. In 1874 they began manufacturing a health corset and from their small beginnings grew the great company of Warner Bros., as famous in Britain as in the U.S.A. and notable as a pioneer of several future innovations in foundationwear.

The return to nature in corsetry was, of course, part of the changing status of women. The whole history of underwear during the past forty or fifty years reflects increasingly the social, psychological and economic effects of what can briefly only be described by the rather outworn word 'emancipation'. This meant that outerwear followed with increasing vigour and enterprise the trend towards freedom in the design and construction of clothes which had begun after the First World War. It also meant that underwear followed suit and that, in practical terms, lightness, comfort and ease were sought in it. Outer clothes became less formal, less fussy and much more uniform. Class distinctions were breaking down. Formality and ostentation were diminishing. The leisured wealthy women no longer dominated fashion in a world where independent working women were on the increase all the time. Spending power was also being spread over a much larger section of the community. The masses were becoming increasingly assertive in expecting their share in all the good things concerned with day-to-day living as well as in the philosophy and politics of existence. Everyone was making for the open-air. Sunbathing became popular and cover-up fashion died. Tennis stars wore knee-length or above-knee divided skirts by the late 1920's. Within a decade shorts were worn for cycling and sport and short skirts were accepted for skating.

These social changes showed themselves in simpler underwear and in the formulation of basics which were mostly established in the 'twenties and have altered little in their general character during the years since then. They were and still are worn in very similar forms by people of all classes everywhere.

The main developments in underwear in general and to a special extent in foundationwear in the period covering the past half century have, however, been due not only to fashion's changes but also to something which had never happened before in the whole history of fashion—nor indeed in the history of mankind. This was a complete revolution in fabrics, consisting of the introduction of a multiplicity of new materials possessed of new properties. These, and the fibres from which they are made, are collectively described as man-made. This term is used generally to describe all fibres and fabrics other than those which have a natural origin, such as wool, cotton, silk and flax.

Man-made fibres are produced entirely by the chemical treatment of certain raw materials, among the chief of which are wood pulp, cotton linters, petroleum extracts and by-products of coal. Such fibres and therefore fabrics are being added to all the time. They have scores of different names, properties and functions and the area of scientific development to which they belong covers the whole of plastics.

The conception of man-made fibres goes far back, although their general use belongs to our time. In 1664 Robert Hooke, an English scientist, suggested in his *Micrographia* that threads could be spun from an 'artificial glutinous composition', following the principle of the silkworm. In 1734 a French scientist, René A. F. de Réaumur, put forward the idea that gums or resins could be drawn out into fibres from which an artificial textile could be produced. But the first known patent for the manufacture of such a fabric was issued in 1855 to George Audemars, a Swiss chemist who had produced fibres from the inner bark of the mulberry and other trees. These he nitrated and dissolved in a mixture of ether and alcohol and then combined with a rubber solution to form a spinning mixture. Rayon, however, to which all this was leading, did not yet become a practical reality. The next step towards this end was taken by Sir Joseph Swan, an Englishman, who started by looking for a better carbon filament for electric light bulbs and in 1883 patented a process for making a filament by squeezing a nitro-cellulose solution into a coagulating medium and then denitrating the filament. He too failed to follow up the textile potentialities of this thread, though the cellulose acetate fibres he produced were crocheted up by his wife and shown at the London Inventions Exhibition of 1885.

The crucial step in developing rayon as a textile was taken about this time by Comte Hilaire de Chardonnet, often called 'the father of the rayon industry'. Beginning his experiments in 1878, he produced his first fibre in 1884 and exhibited articles made from it at the Paris Exposition of 1889. He obtained financial backing for a factory at Besançin in France, where the commercial production of acetate rayon started in 1891. Viscose rayon, which was to be the most successful kind, was the brain-child of three chemists, Cross, Bevan and Beadle, who took out the first patent for it in 1892. It went into production in Britain in 1905 and in 1911 in the U.S.A., with the support of Samuel Courtauld. In 1911 Dr. Dreyfus discovered and patented a method of producing acetate rayon which was developed by British Celanese, the company with which he was associated. It was, however, not until the early 1920's that rayon was of sufficiently good quality, attractive appearance and wearability to go into general use in the clothing and many other industries.

It happens that rayon and many of the man-made fibres subsequently developed have properties particularly suited to underwear. Here they superseded natural materials to a greater extent than in any other section of the clothing industry. The new rayon of the 'twenties very quickly found its way into underwear, and the main reason for this is conveyed by the name 'artificial silk' or 'art silk', which was first given to it. Now largely obsolete as a description and frowned upon by the fabric manufacturers, who rightly credit rayon with new, improved qualities of its own, this description nevertheless explained the instant appeal of rayon in underwear. It brought the luxury look to the assertive new mass market. It made it possible for the ordinary woman of limited means to buy for a price she could afford underwear that closely resembled the real silk and luxury satin that had previously been beyond her means. For the first time she could have pretty, attractively coloured underwear with a soft feel and a flattering cling that had up to that time belonged only to the luxury trade.

The new rayon underwear was by the mid-'twenties being worn by women of all classes, although pure silk, crepe de Chine and satin were to remain an appreciable part of the top end of the trade for nearly twenty years more.

In attractive pastel colours, lace-trimmed and embroidered, rayon opened up a new conception of underwear in general. It was to reign supreme for a generation. It was made in silk, satin, crepe de Chine and other weaves. It also competed vigorously with the expensive knitted silk milanese which was popular in fashionable high-quality underwear. Knitted rayon, which was called locknit, dominated a large section of the mass market in inexpensive underwear for many years, during all the 'thirties and a considerable part of the 'forties. It was the choice of the more down-to-earth section of the public, including a majority of older women who had been used to cotton for most of their lives. Locknit directoire knickers and slips with either built-up shoulders or straps were favoured by the more staid and practical women, while the younger and more fashion-conscious chose fine woven rayons for their French knickers and for lace-trimmed slips that varied comparatively little in shape from those still worn today.

Many of the garments made at this time were in fact not to change greatly for years. Some of them are still recognisably in general wear. They derived from the fashionable styles of the late 'twenties —French knickers, cami-knickers, Princess slips and directoire knickers. All these garments became slimmer and altogether more fitting in style, with a younger look and shorter legs to the knickers and cami-knickers. Much of this slim underwear of the 'thirties was cut on the cross, both in the bust sections and in the skirt or knicker parts of the garments. Diagonal seaming below the bust joined the two sections. *Vogue* in 1938 painted a grotesque picture of pre-bias-cut undies, comparing them to balloons and instancing cami-knickers as a garment in question.

Silk cami-knickers cut on the cross. 1934

Knitted wool continued to be used for vests, as did cotton, and these were less bulky than in the past. Among young people they were frequently worn only in winter or not at all. The brassière and girdle were considered by many people a sufficient first layer of underwear for warmer weather. Combinations were relegated to the elderly, and chemises remained past history.

Although fifteen years after the invention of rayon were to pass before a second and much greater invention in fabrics—that of nylon—was to be achieved, the 'thirties were the most momentous of all periods in history for corsetry. Within that decade the whole conception of corsetry was changed. Materials, components and construction were all revolutionised, although the full fruits of the change were not to be seen until the post-war years, when further developments in man-made fibres added new and exciting chapters to the story.

Flower-printed rayon satin cami-knickers 1945

The big break-through for corsetry in the 'thirties did not, however, come so much from the man-made fibre developments as from a quite different source. This was elastic. Alone and unaided it created a new type of foundation which soon bore no resemblance whatever to the kind that had prevailed continuously, with variations in shape but not in basic construction or materials, for more than three and a half centuries. The new idea almost banished whalebone, steel, lacings, busks, heavy cottons and canvas. It made a clean break with the rigid, stiffened kind of corsetry that had been the only kind ever known.

Zip fastened step-in with figured batiste front panels and stretch-down elastic back. 1935

Elasticity achieved more than this. It brought about a new concept of outer fashion which also had no precedent. Fashion in the years since elastic came into general use in corsetry bears as little resemblance to what it was previously as does electric light to candles or the motor car to the horse carriage. Women could never have taken to relaxed, casual shifts and sweaters, to Chanel-type suits, slacks and trouser suits without supple elasticised foundations underneath. Confronted with the whalebone framework of the old-style corsets our designers of today would have been pipped at the starting post. The soft, figure-following clothes of today would be inconceivable over whaleboned corsets. And the main feature of the curiously confused and almost chaotic 'fashions' of the present time is that, however fantastic some of them are, they are all based on a natural figure—that is, a figure wearing foundationwear that has a 'natural' line. Whether that foundationwear is minimal in support or capable of firm control, the result is still 'natural' and it is created by elastic, natural or man-made.

Unlike the man-made fibres which have been the main influence on other items of underwear in our time, rubber, which is the raw material of natural elastic, is literally as old as the hills, and it was on rubber elastic that the corset revolution was based. The man-made counterparts, usually distinguished from the natural kind by being described as elastomerics, were not developed for practical corsetry purposes until the early nineteen-sixties.

In 1924 pieces of fossilised natural rubber, discovered in lignite deposits in Germany, were dated as belonging to the Eocene period, about 55 million years ago. Natives of Brazil have known of rubber for centuries and it was mentioned by Columbus. Although natural rubber originally came from various wild tropical trees and shrubs, from their roots, branches, leaves and fruit, for practical purposes the rubber tree is the only reliable commercial source. The rubber plantations of the Far East were started from seeds from the Amazon propagated at Kew in a series of experiments which began in 1873, but the large-scale development of the plantations belongs to this century.

The first big step that changed rubber from something merely used for rubbing-out was made by Thomas Hancock, who from 1820 to 1847 worked on the problem of elasticising rubber. He discovered a process of vulcanising it, mainly by the use of sulphur, and took out his first patent in 1820, with fifteen more to follow. This process gave rubber the 'snap back' that elastic means and, by making it resistant to heat and cold, rendered it a workable material. By the mid-nineteenth century this rubber was being used commercially for many purposes, from railway buffers to clothing.

It is an odd fact that although elastic has produced greater changes in corsetry than in any other section of clothing, corsetry was not the first to use it. Credit for this went to the men's footwear trade, which introduced elastic-sided boots in mid-Victorian times, while corsetry remained rigid until well into the present century. There was a parallel with the later use in corsetry: in both cases a rigid article was made stretchable.

An elastic knitted corset was, however, mentioned in the official catalogue of the Great Exhibition at the Crystal Palace in 1851. The same catalogue also describes 'double silk elastic woven corsets, with the royal arms and national emblems inserted . . . woven to fit the body, and recommended for freedom of respiration.' That was a very few years before the tyranny of tight-lacing and the crinoline age started, and these fascinating garments were evidently stillborn. It would be interesting to know more of them.

The first factory for making elastic thread for the boot trade was set up by two brothers, W. & H. Bates, at Leicester in 1863. It widened its scope, but continued under that name until 1925, when it was taken over by the Dunlop Rubber Co. It became the biggest as well as the oldest in Europe and from it has stemmed a major part of important Anglo-American research into elastics, both natural and, more recently, mainly in the last decade, synthetic.

The concept of corsetry in the mid-nineteenth century and the limitations in manufacturing resources in the era of the crinoline and bustle made the association of ideas between elastic and corsetry very remote: so much so that the first recorded corset to be sold with elastic in it is dated 1911. It was called a sports corset—and the elastic was a three-inch band round the waist of a rigid garment.

During the 1914–18 war some elastic was used in wrap-round belts worn by women engaged in strenuous physical war work, which called for freedom as well as control in their corsetry. The first advertisement for a corset without lacing, but with elastic, appeared in the U.S.A. in 1913. In 1914 the 'dancing corset', with elastic in it, also appeared in the U.S.A., then at the height of the tango craze.

Even in the 'twenties, however, the use of elastic in corsetry was very much limited by the fact that the only rubber obtainable was coarse and could be produced only in short lengths. Made on hand-knitting machines, this elastic could be fashioned and made in special shapes, but only to the very limited extent suitable for in-sets, gussets and waistbands in rigid garments. A wrap-round all-rubber corset, made of sheet rubber and called Madame X, appeared in the U.S.A. in 1923 but was short-lived. Similar garments were launched more successfully in the 'thirties, sometimes with the claim that they reduced the figure. The most successful and best-known rubber corset was the Charnaux of the early 1930's, made with perforations and therefore more healthy and comfortable than some others. Sophisticated versions of the idea have been a feature of foundationwear from the 'sixties. One point about these rubber corsets is that for the first time it was advocated that they should be worn next to the skin. Previously corsets had been worn over a chemise or vest and sometimes over petticoats too.

The difficulties regarding rubber elastic in corsetry centred upon the fact that the latex, as the milky sap of the rubber tree was called, coagulated quickly. It was therefore exported at first in hard 'biscuits', then, as the Far East plantations developed, in coagulated sheets. These were reconstituted in this country, being treated with chemicals to give them a 'kick' and then made into sheets about 100 yards long and 36 inches wide. Strips were cut from these and knitted up with rigid yarns for various purposes, including the first uses of elastic in corsetry. It was this shortness of length which limited the use of elastic during the 'twenties.

About 1930 came the big break-through that was to make elastic a basic material of all corsetry. A way was found of exporting the latex emulsion direct from the plantations. With certain processes of concentration and additives, such as ammonia, to prevent spontaneous coagulation, it was shipped in tankers which could carry 200,000 gallons of it, and was sent direct to the factories in sealed drums.

The importation of liquid latex revolutionised the manufacture of elastic thread. An entirely new process of extrusion was used. This process, developed by the Dunlop Rubber Company, meant that very fine elastic thread could be produced in immense lengths. The liquid latex, after going through various processes at the factory, was fed into machines at one end of which were rows of small glass capillary tubes. The mixture flowed through these into acetic acid baths, where it instantly coagulated in the form of continuous parallel rows of round threads. These could have a great variety of thicknesses which were controlled by the size of the nozzles and the rate of the flow. Various other processes followed, with the result that for the first time elastic threads, or Lastex, could be produced in the same lengths as and with similar degrees of fineness to other threads. Therefore these elastic fabrics could now be woven or knitted in substantial lengths and widths. The course of their development in this respect was subject to the process of adapting various kinds of machines to producing elasticised fabrics instead of the rigid ones to which they were accustomed.

The introduction of the new elasticised materials meant a new concept of corsetry. Figure control no longer depended upon boning, lacing and the imposition of a rigid kind of cage on the figure. Instead, support and control were created by means of the special tensions and 'pull' of the elastic in fabrics selected and used by the designer in such a way that they smoothed and moulded the figure by a kind of persuasive action. Health, comfort and appearance all benefited.

The most notable immediate result of the process of extruding rubber elastic was the introduction of the 'roll-on', the most famous corset of its time, with the additional distinction of having added a word to the English language, as well as a new item in the history of underwear. The first roll-on dates from 1932 in Britain and probably a year earlier in the U.S.A. It replaced the hookside or busk-fastening corset for the younger and lighter figures—and for many more too, so great was its comfort. It dominated the 'light control' market for many years. If you belonged to that market you didn't talk of a corset any more; you said a 'roll-on'.

The roll-on was made on the circular knitting machine, which was already being used for elastic, so it was a 'natural' so far as innovations went. One of the main manufacturers of roll-on blanks (the actual 'tubes' without the suspenders) records that his company

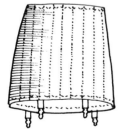

1932 roll-on

began to make them in 1932 and has been making them ever since, though with many improvements. The roll-on was also one of the first arrivals in the imminent new fabrics sphere of two-way stretch which Warner Bros. are recorded as having introduced into corsetry in the U.S.A. in 1932. This was a direct result of the new fine, long elastic threads that were now available.

The 'thirties saw a continuous year-by-year development and variety in corset and brassière materials. These were of two kinds — elasticised and rigid. The latter, although the traditional ones, consisted of a far greater variety of fabrics then we have today. One leading manufacturer who has kept catalogues and actual garments annually since 1931 used, during the 'thirties, grosgrain, four-fold voile, faille, satin, lace, broché, batiste, pekin net, milanese, crepe de Chine, Breton net, Swami, satin brocade, piqué satin, plain and embroidered linen, voile, broderie anglaise, mercerised batiste, brocatelle and delustred satin. At the same time elastic materials were being developed. In 1934 Lastex batiste, hand-knitted elastic and chiffon Lastex yarn are mentioned. In 1935 it is said that 'all the best manufacturers now use Lastex', and nineteen are listed. It is described as 'the wonder yarn.' Among elasticised materials widely used were gripknit, French Lastex-yarn lace, satin Lastex, flowered satin power Lastex yarn, controlastic, aeroknit elastic panels and elastic net. In 1936 these were added to by power lace (lace with elastic power in it), and after a more or less similar picture for 1937, 1938 saw the use of Leno elastic and open-mesh elastic yarns. Woven elastics were added about 1939 and marked a big technical advance, but advantage could not be taken of the possibilities they opened up until after the 1939–45 War.

During these pre-war years corsetry styles moved over steadily from busk-front and hookside wrap-ons to step-ins, semi-step-ins and corselettes. For younger and lighter women the roll-on was well to the fore. Laced-up garments were disappearing from ranges with any claim to fashion. Although in the early 'thirties moderate and, to a smaller extent, heavy boning persisted, it also was decreasing as elastics became more adaptable and versatile. Double material and stitching also often replaced bones as a means of firming garments. Figures were becoming more shapely, but with softer contours than in the past. In 1935, C. B. Cochran declared that his Young Ladies should have curves and the Young Ladies of the famous impresario of the 'thirties were the figure and fashion ideal of the time.

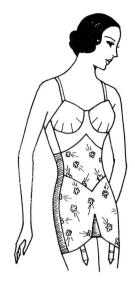

Backless corselette in figured batiste with swami brassière top c.1935

Aertex girdle. 1938

Brassière in satin and lace. 1940

Brassière in net with stitched satin undercups. 1940

Long brassière in lace-trimmed batiste, with suspenders. 1940

The 'thirties were years of backless evening dresses and many corselettes are described as being backless. By 1938 many were 'backless and boneless'. Stretch-down back panels became prominent in the later 'thirties. 1936 saw an all-elastic corselette with special two-way stretch panels both back and front. By 1939 most girdles were either step-ins or semi-step-ins, but the earlier hook-side wrap-on styles persisted, and the traditional rigid corsetry, with its back-lacing, front busk and numerous bones, continued to be in production, though on a steadily diminishing scale. It is still not entirely dead. It is only within very recent years that at least one major manufacturer closed down the 'rigid section', which a few others still maintain.

All through the 'thirties the predominant corset and brassière colours were pink or peach or variations on these tones, described as rose-beige, tea rose, apricot and other similar names. A very few garments were made in white, but other colours almost disappeared and black was very much in the luxury class.

An unexpected feature of corsetry of the 'thirties was the existence of garments at what even today would be a high price. In 1931 a corselette in peach satin and lace cost eight guineas—which in today's terms would be many times that amount. This was from the range of Berlei, a manufacturer who also sold garments priced in shillings. Among other items of the early 'thirties were corselettes, again in satin, in white, peach or pink, with lace and hand-knit elastic and a lace frill at the bottom, at six and a half guineas. In 1935 luxury was expressed in a 'de luxe semi-step-in controlette in black Lastex-yarn satin, specially lifted bust section in Alenôon lace'. One step-in girdle in 1936 cost £5, and six guineas was the 1937 price of a 'de luxe' evening corselette in black satin with velvet appliqué on torso, modern uplift bustline and hand-knit elastic. Another surprising feature of old catalogues is the number of garments in the ranges. One company had 104 different brassières on its list in the mid-'thirties, plus many dozens of belts and corselettes.

In review, the most remarkable thing about the underwear of the 'thirties was the extent to which it either created the styles and characteristics that still persist or else, particularly in foundation-wear, anticipated developments generally associated with the post-war years, and especially with the 'fifties. Many of the innovations related to the brassière. This was described in the 'thirties as having cup busts, defined busts, uplift busts and even an accentuated bustline. In 1935 in the U.S.A. Warner Bros. introduced cup fittings for the first time. They had realised what now seems a very self-evident fact—that the measurement of the bust and the size of the breasts involve two different measurements, if the latter are to be accorded their 'natural' shape, and that the brassière must be designed to take both requirements into account. In this innovation there were four cup sizes, A. B. C. and D., just as today. It was, however, some years before this system and the descriptions were generally adopted. Up to 1940 bust sizes alone were still being widely used in Britain, although descriptive sizes of bust cups were on record, in 1939, under the names junior, medium, full and full with wide waist.

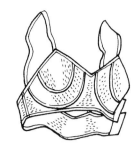

Side fastening brassière in Pekin net. 1935

The strapless bra was introduced in 1938, but although this anticipated its great success in the 1950's it did not succeed and it disappeared for many years. The wired bra, also due to take an important place from the 'fifties right up to the present, likewise made its first appearance in the immediate pre-war years. Examples of it are recorded in Britain in 1938, but it was not successfully established until the early 'fifties, when improvements in materials, techniques and design made it a highly favoured style. The first padded bra dated from the mid- thirties and inset foam pads were used by 1940.

The high bosom of post-war years appeared in 1939 bras and corselettes. The pointed bust and the exaggeration of the shape of the bust, also associated closely with the 1950's, originated in the Mae West era of the late 'twenties and 'thirties. Highly emphasised bust cups were created by means of circular stitching, another device familiar in the 'fifties, and also by stiffening inserted into the points of the cups. At both periods the emphasis on the bust was exploited by the film world. Bra-slips were also produced in the 'thirties. In 1932 in America Maidenform combined a brief bra with a slip to produce a 'costume slip'. This was the prototype of the bra-slip, which was to become an important part of the general range of underwear in the later 'sixties. Similar garments also appeared in Britain in the thirties. Spiral boning, an important innovation and amenity in corsetry and still part of contemporary foundationwear, first came into use in 1938.

Although the patent for the slide fastener was taken out in America in 1914, it was many years before it developed even there and it first appeared in corsetry in 1931. In Britain the 'Lightning' zip arrived in 1933–4. It was soon being used by leading corset manufacturers. In 1935 salesgirls were advised, in a trade publication, to 'explain its use and operation' to their customers. To start with the zip was heavy and much-taped, and to the post-war years belong its more sophisticated developments, such as self-locking slides and much finer constructions.

The pantee girdle, which in its many forms dominates the foundationwear scene today, was acclaimed in 1935. 'The pantee corset', said *Corsetry & Underwear* in June of that year, 'is sweeping triumphantly into the best-seller class of leading fashion houses and is destined to make fashion history'. It was a true prophecy. One successful 1935 style was the 'Silcute' by Kestos, a two-way stretch elastic pantee made in pure Lastex yarn, fashioned to shape and with a smooth surface free of seams or bones. There were also many other versions in the immediate pre-war years.

Just before the 1939 war broke out, there was evidence of a return to fashions that emphasised the waist. *Vogue* wrote enthusiastically: 'The only thing you must have . . . is a tiny waist, held in if necessary by super-light-weight boned and laced corsets. There isn't a silhouette in Paris that doesn't cave in at the waist'. Also advocated is 'an old-fashioned boned and laced corset, made, by modern magic, light and persuasive as a whisper'. Although the war put an end to that trend, the first real post-war fashion, the Dior 'New Look', did require 'a tiny waist' and was worn with a corset that assisted this. It was as though fashion had been put in a deep freeze for the intervening years.

9 | *The Man-made Fibres Revolution: 1939–1971*

Nylon, which is the most important innovation in the whole history of underwear, also originated in the immediate pre-war years, although its use in underwear, as in outer clothing and numerous other commodities, is a post-war story.

E. I. Du Pont de Nemours Inc. were the originators of nylon, and they gave it its name (a generic one, coined by them and not based on any existent word). Nylon, a polyamide derived from carbon, oxygen and hydrogen, was the result of a fundamental research programme started by Du Pont in 1927 and carried out by the late Dr. Wallace H. Carothers and his staff. The aim of the research was not to create a specific product but to study polymerisation—how and why very small molecules join up and form large ones. By 1930 Dr. Carothers and his researchers had discovered that a fibre of extreme tensile strength could be drawn from a treacle-like mass of linear polymers, but years of research followed and Dr. Carothers died in 1937, a year before the discovery of nylon was announced by Du Pont in October 1938.

World-wide interest was roused when the Company showed the first ever nylon stockings at the New York World Fair in that year. About 27 million dollars had in the previous eleven years been spent on research and development and fantastic claims were inevitably made for the new nylon, most of which Du Pont had to disclaim. The first nylon stockings were offered for sale to employees of the Company at its experimental station at Wilmington, Delaware, in February 1939. In the same month similar stockings were exhibited at the Golden Gate International Exposition in San Francisco and in March the first public sales took place at a few retail stores at Wilmington. The first large public sales on a country-wide scale, were made in October 1939.

The first complete outfit made of nylon was shown at the New York World's Fair in 1940. Nylon apparel then began to appear on the American market in wider variety but in limited quantities. It included women's lingerie and foundation garments and it was widely acclaimed by the public. Its heyday, however, was brief, for in February 1942 nylon in America went to war, just as it had done in Britain two years before.

By a strange coincidence nylon, which was to have a profound effect upon the future of all clothing, was introduced into Britain on January 1, 1940, the day when wartime restrictions first hit the country in the way in which traditionally it hurts most—by the introduction of food rationing.

On this January 1, British Nylon Spinners Ltd., a private Company, with a capital of £300,000 subscribed in equal proportions by I.C.I. Ltd. and Courtaulds Ltd., was formed to manufacture and sell nylon in Britain. This was possible because Du Pont had granted nylon rights in Britain to I.C.I., who in turn granted them to British Nylon Spinners and Courtaulds.

Needless to say, Britain's first five years' output of the new yarn went wholly to such vital wartime needs as parachutes, jungle tents, glider tow-ropes and tarpaulins. For these nylon was an incomparable and almost incredibly opportune invention, because of its unequalled strength. British women's first personal experience of nylon came in the shape of a thin trickle of stockings brought back privately from the U.S.A. in the early war years, mainly by Atlantic-crossing business men. The sheer-clad legs of the lucky few were the bitter envy of their less fortunate sisters.

The reason for this envy was not solely because of the marvels of nylon. Stockings soon began to be in short supply. Food shortages were inevitably accompanied by other shortages in both the materials and the labour needed for civilian production. As early as Spring 1940 controls were, for instance, introduced restricting the amount of corsetry available for civilian use to 75% of the pre-war level of the manufacturer concerned.

On May 31st 1941 clothes rationing came into force in Britain with the Government's Utility scheme and the long-to-be-familiar CC41 symbol. This meant that only certain specified cloths could be used for clothing. Ceiling prices and profit margins for all types of garments were drastically curtailed. The larger proportion of garments was price-controlled. Only a limited amount of regular standard merchandise, called general quota and not price-controlled, could be made. Many manufacturers found themselves caught up in concentration schemes with others who would normally be competitors. It also became increasingly difficult to obtain the innumerable components required for the production of clothing even on a restricted scale. In corsetry, for instance, steel supports were for obvious reasons obtainable only in very small quantities and fibre had to be substituted. Imports of rubber for corsetry and underwear elastics were also hit.

The introduction of the clothing rationing system in Britain, with coupons that had to be given up for every item, was aimed at preventing unfairness in the distribution of the limited supplies of garments available in every category, but it also inevitably hampered development and brought fashion largely to a standstill for years. How long the wartime restrictions lasted is apt to be forgotten. They continued long after hostilities had ended. The scheme for clothes rationing in general went on until March 1949 and it was not until then that any real easing began. Even after that restrictions remained. The Utility Scheme, aimed at ensuring the production of necessary clothing requirements under price-controlled conditions, lasted until 1952 and the subsequent controls exercised by the D scheme over manufacturing and selling continued until 1955. Within this elaborate framework of clothing restrictions only very limited quantities of garments of higher quality and price were permitted for many years and to find them was a kind of treasure hunt. The process of relaxation came slowly.

In corsetry both in Britain and in America one beam of light shone through the darkness created by the low standards imposed on manufacturers and their fabric suppliers by Government departments. In Britain women in the services and the hosts of others required to do 'men's work' and to stand for long hours at factory benches were vocal on the fact that they now needed good corsetry more than ever for physical support. These clamorous voices eventually reached the ears of the Government early in 1944 through a recently established body, The Corset Guild of Great Britain, formed in 1943 by retail shop buyers who were, of course, the direct recipients of the public's pleas. With the support of a number of leading corset manufacturers, who had joined them in the Guild, they presented at 10 Downing Street a petition on behalf of British women. This resulted in March 1944 in corsetry being classified under what was known as the 'Essential Works Order'. This enabled the corset industry to maintain certain standards and to produce garments that were functionally designed and capable of being comfortable and providing support for the figure.

In America similar agitation arose, and there too it achieved a successful result. Women in America had the advantage of a staunch advocate in high office—Miss Mary Anderson, Director of the Women's Bureau of the Department of Labour. She declared corsets to be essential to the performance of women's tasks in the war effort, pointing out that fatigue was the main reason why women frequently left their war jobs in the U.S.A. To provide good corsets, which would reduce fatigue, was therefore necessary to the vigorous maintenance of the war effort.

After the war America, less subject than Britain to prolonged shortages and general stringency, secured a considerable lead in many fields of civilian production. Not least of these were those of corsetry and underwear, where both in materials and in design Britain lagged behind for many years.

The process of easing women out of wartime restrictions was given a bold impetus by the introduction of the famous 'New Look' in Paris by Christian Dior in Spring 1947 in the first collection shown at his newly-established couture house. While cloth was still rationed he put yards of it into full, flowing, below-calf-length skirts, extending to twelve inches from the ground and replacing the shorter, tubular styles that had been established for years. Instead of the current square-shouldered jackets with lightly defined waists he presented a short jacket with rounded shoulders and a nipped-in waist. The padding hitherto used for the very wide, squared shoulders now gave shape to the slightly flared basques of the new Dior jackets.

In spite of the loud disapproval of the British authorities (headed by Mr. Harold Wilson as president of the Board of Trade), and protests from the patriotic and the serious-minded, the new line was instantly and widely adopted in Britain. Fashion came to life again, and designers, both in couture houses and among the wholesale manufacturers, seized upon it with the heady excitement that came from years of frustration and repression. Though the initial extreme New Look was soon modified for general wear, it established a trend that lasted for nearly ten years, until the middle nineteen-fifties.

Under the new full skirts went voluminous petticoats and in the first enthusiasm these were often brightly coloured and frilled. In many cases they were trophies rescued from grandmother's attic. There was a fine *cachet* in letting a flash of scarlet or bright green

'New Look' petticoat and matching boned corselette 1948

silk be glimpsed as these busy, active post-war women swung on to buses and trains in their unsuitable but exhilarating new flowing skirts.

To make the most of the newly revived small waist, the 'waspie' appeared. This was a short corset, sometimes only five or six inches deep, made of rigid material with elastic inserts, little bones and sometimes back lacing. It was shaped sharply into the waist and was worn very tight, in the manner of the despised Victorians. Other corsets of the time also showed an hour-glass look. The idea was not, however, widely adopted or long-lived. The very fashionable essayed it. Model girls groaningly laced or pulled themselves into tight 'waspies' for fashion shows, but once the parade was over off came the new menace: their corsets were killing them. Usually the short waspie was worn over the familiar roll-on or a light pantee-girdle.

From this time underwear in general was transformed by the use of nylon, which began to be used in increasing quantities. There is a curious footnote to its wartime rôle in the advertisement in April 1946 of a famous brassière company which refers to 'parachute fabric into Partos brassières, creating beauty and with their scientific design ensuring lasting satisfaction.' Nylon was, however, being 'demobbed' and in 1947 it was first shown at the British Industries Fair, where the new underwear fabrics made from it were described as 'a beauty and a revolution.' Nylon foundation garments

Boned back-lacing 'Waspie' in nylon and satin with elastic satin side panels. 1948

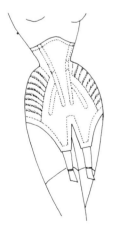

High fashion 'Waspie' girdle in heavy satin with padded hips and back lacing 1947

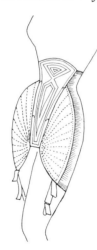

Satin girdle with side sections of elastic. 1947

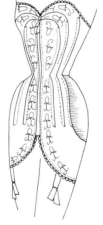

1947 'New Look' evening corset in embroidered satin with elastic insets on hips and slide front fastener

Calf-length nylon slip trimmed at bust and hem with lace and pleated nylon insertion and frill. 1957

and lingerie were included in the garments shown, among the underwear being items of the warp-knit type material which, as nylon tricot, was to occupy a dominant position in the underwear world from that time onwards until the present day.

Nylon did indeed introduce a new era in the underwear world. Delectable, gossamer-light, hard-wearing fabrics that could be rinsed out and drip-dried in an hour or two, with no need of ironing, were now available on the mass market, at prices that would previously have bought only coarse and unattractive garments. A wide choice of nylon materials now came into existence, in different weights as well as in various knitted and woven constructions. In the knitted type, the weight and texture were and still are indicated in two ways. The word denier, also used for elastic nets, means the weight in grammes of 9000 metres of synthetic fibre in the form of a continuous filament. Deniers can vary from 15 for stockings to as much as 140 to 1120 for heavy stable and elastic materials. Another variation is described as gauge, here again for elastics as well as nylon. It means the number of ends of the yarn on a knitting machine to each inch of fabric. The higher the gauge the finer the material.

Crepe slip with side zip. 1949 and Crepe slip trimmed with embroidered net and ribbon bows. 1949

'Combinations' in crepe with brassière-shaped top trimmed with lace c.1946

Chemise-culotte in crepe satin, trimmed with Point-de-Paris c.1946

The attraction and availability of nylon and its inexpensiveness were so great that underwear, which had hitherto been even more susceptible to social and fashion snobbery than had outerwear, now became almost classless. The new nylons were not suitable for hand-sewing, so the vogue for hand-made silk, satin and crepe de Chine underwear among elegant women came to an end. Underwear became truly democratic, in which respect it preceded a similar trend in outerwear that has become manifest in recent years.

Although by today's standards the underwear of the late 'forties and early 'fifties seems voluminous and fussy, the introduction of nylon and of the mass-production methods that were stimulated by the rising demand for what was now a machine-made article, progressively led to simpler and more functional styles. Briefs, in various kinds of nylon and in many designs, superseded the more elaborate French knickers of pre-war glamour. Cami-knickers went out of fashion and the simpler slip was worn. Underwear, which had been cut on the cross when woven silks were used, was now usually cut on the straight, as befitted the knitted fabrics that were mainly used.

At the same time that it was introducing a new concept in underwear, nylon also had a profound effect on foundationwear. The cottons, brochés, satins and other fabrics previously needed to ensure control in rigid garments or parts of garments could now be replaced by lightweight nylon taffeta, nylon voile, nylon marquisette and similar materials. As strong as natural ones but immeasurably lighter, they were being used in corsetry by 1947 and they contributed an important step towards the glamorising of foundationwear and the creation of lightweight garments capable of providing degrees of control hitherto available only by the use of formidable materials. Even more important was the contribution made by nylon elastic net towards the lightening of foundationwear.

Important too was the great improvement in elasticised materials brought about by the production of them on the warp knitting machine, which began in the early 1950's. Originally bobbinet machines were used for these fabrics and subsequently various other lace machines were also employed. The original patent for two-way stretch fabrics made on warp knitting looms was taken out in the nineteenth century, but it was not until after the 1939–44 War that the high production potential of these machines was

Nylon slip and pantie set trimmed with scalloped lace with ruched nylon insertion. 1958

Power net pantee with lightly boned satin front panel, worn with nylon bra inset with elastic net in front. 1948

Terylene bra with pointed circle-stitched cups. 1957

Back-fastening long bra in nylon and lace with elastic batiste sides and centre back and stitched, stiffened cups. 1957

Nylon 'Sweater Girl' bra with wide, pointed circle-stitched cups. 1957

recognised. Their development started in the U.S.A., and reached Britain in the early 1950's. The main advantages of the warp knitting machine, previously used for locknit materials, were far greater speed and far longer runs of material. Where previously the length of elastic net that could be woven was limited by the amount of elastic that could be run on—and off—a bobbin, the new process meant that several hundred yards of material could be produced continuously, as opposed to the previous fifteen or sixteen yards. Production capacity for two-way stretch fabrics increased enormously and also resulted in much cheaper fabrics.

The full effect of this on corset design and manufacture was not, however, realised until about 1954–5, when the fully elasticised foundation garment broke through into the popular market. A pioneer in this development was the famous 'Little X' by Silhouette, the first two-way stretch corset to be marketed in Britain under a brand name of its own. It was rapidly followed by a series of other branded all-elastic garments. From that time onwards the conception of the all-elastic corset was firmly established.

The item of underwear with the liveliest history in the post-war years is the brassière. It had, it will be recalled, gone through quite a variety of developments in the 'thirties, first in the Mae West era and later, when the Scarlett O'Hara bra had quite a vogue in America. This lead from Hollywood characterised fashion developments after the war, when American films dominated the entertainment world. In addition, America's briefer participation in the war and her more rapid material recovery gave her, among other things, a good lead in the development of the man-made fibres that were particularly important in this connection.

Reasons given for the exploitation of the bosom in post-war years include the suggestion that 'In the hungry post-1939 world, as in the hungry post-Napoleonic world . . . the female breast is the obvious symbol of nourishment.' Another view is that it was simply a shift of the erogenous zone. Dior's 'New Look' of 1947 emphasised the bosom, together with other feminine curves, so it was not strange that women everywhere became very bra-conscious. American film stars in the 'forties and even in the 'fifties are credited with having risen to fame by virtue of the splendour of their bosoms rather than of their talents and it was declared that 'one American lady was selected to star in a popular American television programme entirely on account of her oversize bosom.'

How serious the correct fashionable shape of the bust was is instanced by a dramatic episode in the best-selling novel *The Carpet Baggers*. Believed to have its origin in fact, it tells how a very curvaceous Hollywood actress, about to be launched on her first starring rôle, was encased in a brassière that made her into a straight line, and then in a harness-style bra that was little better. Unfortunately, without a bra, her ample bosom bounced. The fashion designer revolted, declaring she was 'a designer, not a structural engineer.' That gave the director the vital clue. An aeronautical engineer was sent for and, with the aid of calipers to measure the depth and circumference, and calculations to find the point of stress, he designed a bra on the suspension principle in a little over an hour. The result was perfect and sensationally successful.

The most popular type of bra in the 'fifties was known as the 'sweater girl' bra, which reached its peak (literally) about 1957. Inspired by film star Jane Russell, its aim was to create an exaggerated high, pointed bosom—an achievement in which nature was almost wholly replaced by artifice. These bras were shaped to sharp points, stiffened and built up. For those to whom Nature had been niggardly, 'falsies' or padded bras of this shape were the answer. 'The ideal aimed at', says Pearl Binder, a well-known writer on the history of fashion, 'is two spiked cones never before seen in Europe and related only to the female form in African sculpture.'

This trend was so generally followed that in 1955 leading corset buyers attending a conference of the Corset Guild of Great Britain at Manchester dwelt on the fact that three out of every four women were at that time wearing 'cuties' and 'falsies'—both descriptions of the artificial bust-maker. All sorts of bust-improvers were advertised and displayed in shop windows, including pneumatic busts that could be inflated at will, like a balloon.

Wiring was revived about 1945, and though at first hard, uncomfortable and suspected in some quarters of being dangerous to the breast, it was in a few years flat, light, well-covered and perfectly comfortable to wear. Circular stitching was widely used to achieve those fashionable protruding, pointed bust cups.

Another development of the 'fifties was the strapless bra, which was very widely worn with the strapless evening dresses which remained in vogue for many years. Such dresses usually had full skirts, which were held out either by wiring, in a revival of the

Strapless evening corselette with foam-lined cups. 1960

Long-line strapless bra in nylon taffeta with elastic net insets and lace trimming. 1960

Short strapless bra contoured with foam rubber. 1960

Bouffant waist petticoat in ruched nylon, mounted on paper nylon base with scalloped hemline and under-frills of net. 1959

Waist petticoat in nylon with frills made of 50 yards lace-edged nylon net. 1959

Waist slip in paper nylon with flaring over-skirt of fine nylon and slotted ribbon. 1957

crinoline, or by petticoats of stiffened materials, including tiers of nylon net. The very full crinolines were mainly worn on very formal occasions and by the wealthy and fashionable, and the Royal Ladies wore them with great faithfulness for many years.

There was, also, in the late 1950's, a dominating 'young' fashion for short, very full daytime skirts of the dirndl type. Under these were worn petticoats of almost ballerina fullness, belling out with rows upon rows of frills and lace. Sometimes they even reverted to the old-fashioned embroidered or lace-trimmed starched cotton. Sometimes they were of stiffened nylon net. Under them briefs were functionally plain, but bras still aimed at uplift, and the bosom was emphasised by padding and wiring, though this was moderating towards the end of the 1950's. In corsetry the step in, in elastic net, was favoured by the young. The corselette was in considerable favour, but, in spite of the stimulus given to designers by nylon and improvements in the making of elastic nets, it was still a fairly heavy garment. So were the numerous functional girdles that controlled curves and trimmed outlines under fashions that were much more formal and figure-fitting than those of the late 'sixties and early 'seventies.

Waist petticoat in hand-painted paper nylon with two net under-skirts. 1960

Foundationwear was enjoying a boom at this time and an Economist Intelligence Unit Survey showed that sales of foundation garments in Britain practically doubled between 1948 and 1958. For foundationwear, moreover, there was about to come a new revolution as momentous in its sphere as that which nylon had produced in the lingerie world. The source of change was again to be a man-made fibre, and its impact is still being strongly felt today.

This latest innovation, still in its heyday, and still developing, was the invention of man-made elastics. Generically described as Spandex fibres, they contain no natural rubber at all and have become known as elastomerics. Lycra, which dominates this group of fibres, is, like nylon, much lighter than its natural counterpart. Weight by weight, it is about three times as powerful as rubber elastic, so it has opened up a new conception of light-weight, yet controlling foundationwear.

Lycra, like nylon, was invented in the Du Pont U.S.A. Laboratories, this time in the course of research aimed at finding ways of producing a fibre that would have the elastic qualities of rubber but at the same time be a true textile. This project led to the discovery of what was known in its experimental stages as Fibre K. It was introduced for trade evaluation in the U.S.A. in 1958. In October 1959 the trade name 'Lycra' was announced. A pilot plant started producing Lycra in America and foundationwear manufacturers began to put it into production so as to test the product and its potential market. In December 1960 fabric made from the new fibre was described in *Corsetry & Underwear* in Britain, and in the same month Warner Bros. launched out with a full-page British trade advertisement for their first garment 'in the new Lycra fabric', a step-in called 'Little Godiva'. In the next month their 'Merry Widow' evening corselette with Lycra was introduced into Britain.

In 1961 Warners again made foundationwear history by introducing into Britain their 'Birthday Suit', a close-fitting, smoothly knitted pantee-corselette, using Lycra, boneless, almost seamless and rather like a swimsuit. Made in sizes 34 to 38 , it weighed a mere three ounces but cost the considerable sum of $8\frac{1}{2}$ guineas. It was the forerunner of the 'nude look' that was to make headlines a few years later and also of many future body stockings and similar garments of the late 'sixties and early 'seventies. All of these were the culmination of a new simplification of foundationwear made possible by Lycra.

In January 1962 it was said that 'Spandex fibres are currently bringing about a revolution in the foundation garment industry' and in that year an American plant went into commercial production.

Strapless corselette in nylon ninon and nylon elastic net, hooked at back. 1957

The original 'Birthday Suit' 1961

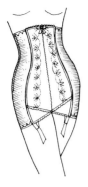

High-line semi-step-in in Lycra elastic net with satin stretch-down back panel and fold-back front of embroidered nylon marquisette. 1964

In November 1962 Du Pont celebrated this in London by holding a spectacular parade of foundationwear that used Lycra. At the end of 1963 'everything is coming up in Lycra for the Spring'.

In 1963 a plant for manufacturing Lycra fibre was built at Dordrecht in the Netherlands, mainly to supply the European market, including Britain, which had up to then been dependent upon imports from the U.S.A. or Canada. In August 1969, when Lycra had become a mainstay of British fashion foundationwear, further production was started at Du Pont's plant at Maydown, Londonderry, which was already engaged in producing Orlon acrylic fibre. The major part of the Lycra made here was for the supply of the United Kingdom and European Free Trade Area countries.

For the first few years, foundationwear with Lycra mostly made use of nets, produced in a large variety of deniers, as were natural rubber elastic fabrics and nylon. Such fabrics did not consist entirely of Lycra, any more than their conventional counterparts were wholly of rubber elastic. The proportion of Lycra (which usually ranged from 15% to 40%) was dependent upon the amount of stretch required.

The new fabrics containing Lycra were comfortably supple in texture. The lightness of the fibre was a prime attraction and its special qualities included the possession of from two to four times the break-strength of natural elastic thread of the same denier and up to twice the recovery power. It was also claimed to have better resistance to abrasion. It resisted perspiration, oils and lotions and was unharmed by detergents. It could be dyed. Unlike conventional rubber elastic, Lycra could be knitted into fabrics in its bare state as well as covered, and this meant that it opened the way to new fabric constructions, which were soon to be developed. From the start it meant a new era of light-weight control for foundationwear.

The general trend of foundations from the 'sixties to the present time has been progressively towards increasingly natural shaping. It has aimed at smoothing and controlling the figure and improving on nature without exaggerating natural curves or introducing any artificiality. Where muscles are weak, where the figure is flabby and has lost its ideal tautness, the foundation garment of today takes over and persuades it back towards what it should be.

The adoption of fabrics made with Lycra and the consequent production of new, supple light-weight controlling foundation

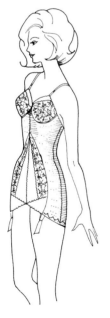

Corselette in Lycra elastic net, front panel in nylon lace and marquisette. 1963

garments that promoted a natural line of a kind hitherto impossible to achieve, coincided with an unprecedented breakaway of outer fashion from the conventional course it had followed for some hundreds of years. The 'permissive' society of the recent 'sixties adopted 'permissive' clothes. The traditions of couture, the fashion leadership of the wealthy and socially prominent and the conventions of dress were supplanted by the 'anything goes' mood of the young and trendy. The result was a complete break from the previous sequence of fashion history, and confusion in the fashion trade.

But amid the confusion there has been one constant fact. Whatever the vageries and eccentricities of outerwear, the shape beneath has been a natural one. And only foundations made with today's materials could bring to the figure the natural kind of control that fashion from the 'sixties has demanded.

That this is so raises a kind of hen-and-egg quandary. Which came first? The 'natural' foundation garments or the permissive outer ones? The recent shifts and mini-skirts, the newer softly shaped midis, the trouser suits, caftans and unisex clothes could not have been worn without unsightliness by any but a tiny minority of women in an age of corsets made of heavy rigid materials reinforced with whalebone and steel, stiffened by busks and fiercely laced into the desired shape.

The interdependence of outer clothes and underwear, specially corsets, through the centuries is an intriguing speculation. Farthingales, panniers, crinolines and bustles all had their appropriate underpinnings. But these came from natural materials that were there for the finder. How can we explain the more than providential fact that scientists in their laboratories invented elastomeric fibres at precisely the time when they dovetailed neatly into the trend of fashion for ease and naturalness? How line up Lycra with that dress revolution which fashion historian James Laver regards as 'probably an irreversible wave of female emancipation', such as has never happened before?

The chief recent development of Lycra has been in the production of tricot types of fabric. With the look of soft satin, these have made three important contributions to the underwear story. First, the garments made from them are attractive to a degree that foundation-wear has never previously attained. Secondly, they opened the way to the use of printed materials which, although they date from 1961,

1968—71 co-ordinates in printed tricot with Lycra and printed nylon tricot

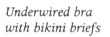

Underwired bra with bikini briefs

Bra with fibre-fill cups, worn with matching short petticoat

Mid-length pantee with wired bra.

Bra-slip with fibre-fill cups and elastic inset at back

Natural line bra and matching bikini briefs in nylon tricot. 1968

did not enjoy their full vogue or look fully effective until the new fabrics were available. Thirdly, as tricots with Lycra can be matched by stable tricots, they led the way to co-ordinates—matching groups of pantees, step-ins, bras, briefs and slips, with stretch fabric used where needed and non-stretch elsewhere. Co-ordinates were in existence by 1962, but did not become prominent until the late 'sixties, when they were chiefly sought in prints. The indications at the start of the 'seventies are that prints have passed their peak and that self-colours are superseding them, but that match-making is still going strong in the underwear world.

Among the recent fashions that have influenced underwear the most important was the mini-skirt. It was at its height (literally) from 1967 until well into 1969, when a violent winter-time swing to the maxi dealt it a strong, if partial, body-blow. From these two extremes there emerged, half way through 1970, the midi-length, coming to varying points on the calf. The importance of this lies not in a mere juggling with hemlines, but in the fact that it expresses a new, softer, more feminine look, a shapely figure with a defined natural waistline and something like a return to elegance. It indicates a reaction from blatant, defiant freedom and has social echoes in the contemporary trend of thought. It is also, for a change, a fashion for all ages, not only for the young.

The mini was outstanding in the fact that for the first time ever it revealed female limbs up to and including the thighs. Previously the knees had been the limit—and when they were unveiled for the first time less than fifty years ago that was the word which horrified older and more staid people applied to the fashion. The progressive revelation of the female body has, however, been proceeding briskly in fashions of recent years, with general acceptance.

So far as underwear was concerned the mini made stockings, established for centuries, an outmoded idea because they stopped short of the newly-exposed thighs. With them the suspender, proud achievement of less than a century ago, also met its Waterloo. Tights, more reminiscent of fifteenth- and sixteenth-century male fashion than of anything in the woman's world, took over. With them the pantee-girdle and pantee-corselette became the new foundationwear classics. The girdle and corselette thus became two-legged. That is still the latest underwear revolution and the crystal ball does not reveal anything beyond it. Following the lines of the

Pantee-corselette in Lycra and nylon lace. 1970

Long-line pantee in Lycra elastic net with firm front panel. 1967

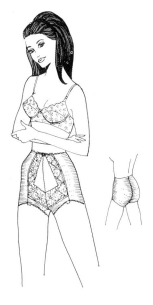

Similar short leg pantee-girdle with shaped back seam for natural line. 1967

body as closely as any garment could, these new underpinnings have brought the wheel full cycle from the whalebone stays of history. To complete the cycle, even the word 'corset' now fails to describe the pantees, pantee-corselettes and girdles that are generally worn. The word foundationwear is the most acceptable of the suggestions made in the search for a suitable description, and a number of leading stores have re-named their corset departments 'foundation-wear departments.' Other verbal innovations include 'under-fashions' and 'body fashions', but both are too generally applicable to underwear to replace the word 'corset' which remains irre-placeable and therefore now much more needed than is the traditional form of the garment itself.

Another first-ever in underwear history was the 'see-through' look which started in the mid-'sixties and has persisted ever since, though on a very limited scale. It came after the 1963 shock fashion of the topless dress. Although this complete bare-bosom style was rarely worn and then only by the sensation-seeking and the exhibitionists, it was taken seriously enough to be banned by fifty-seven Mecca dance halls in 1964. Its successor, the see-through fashion, is ambiguous and more persistent. Its shock effect has been repeated in successive seasonal fashion shows. At its literal extreme it means a transparent blouse or dress worn without any bra or other underwear on the upper part of the body. In practice it is more usual for a skin-tone bra or body-stocking to be worn.

Behind this there is something new in underwear history. Rarely before has underwear been meant to be seen—except for the frilled neckline of the chemise glimpsed above the dress in the seventeenth century, the chemise sleeves peering below the cuffs or through the slashed sleeves of the same period and the petticoats revealed by the looped-up skirts of the seventeenth and eighteenth centuries. These last, at their peak about 1720, *were*, designed to be seen and were accordingly made of fabrics often richer than the accompany-ing outerwear.

Today it is a very practical possibility that underwear will be-come even more visible. The original purposes of underwear, made of washable linen or cotton, were to protect the body from outer-wear which was not washable and to protect outerwear from the body which, until Victorian times, did not know the daily bath—or anything like it. In addition, as fashion became more elaborate, from Elizabethan times onwards, underwear contributed to the shape of it by means of padding, boning, farthingales, hoops, crinolines and other cage-like structures. All these were intended to be an invisible kind of upholstery for the body.

Now all this is changed. Man-made elastomerics and other fabrics control the figure and enhance its shape, but look as attractive as fashionable outerwear. The use of man-made materials for all purposes means that much outerwear is as washable, drip-dry and non-iron, as underwear. There is therefore no reason why underwear and outerwear should not merge. Already this has been started by the bra dress, a two-in-one which has its own built-in bra. The jump-suit for casual wear can also be a complete outfit, underwear and outerwear in one. Manufacturers have produced various other casuals in stretch fabrics, with built-in control for busts, waists and hips, so that they are complete in themselves and need no additions.

This idea of casual or leisure wear, which looks like joining up underwear and outerwear, is not new in our time. It was known in the late nineteenth century, when tea gowns, worn without corsets, were favoured for elegant relaxation. In 1925 Chanel anticipated much future fashion in this sphere (as in others) with lounging pyjamas, an example of which can be seen at the Victoria & Albert Museum. Very alluring in pink, petunia and purple silk, they have flowing petal-like sleeves and a highly intricate two-tier construction of very tight pyjama legs under very full ones. This kind of half-way-house dressing has come much to the fore recently, in forms varying today from certain kinds of trouser suits to caftans and djellabas, from cat-suits to combined foundation/sunbathing/beachwear. Young designers at the Leicester Polytechnic's department of foundationwear and lingerie design (the only source of such specialised training in Europe) show a strong trend towards combining underwear and outerwear. The gorgeously embroidered top of an evening dress is really a bra. The pantee-corselette in patterned, coloured fabrics half-revealed by the overdress. Under and outer harmonise, blend, play hide-and-seek with each other.

10 | Milestones in Manufacture

It is a confusing and disturbing experience to stand back and try to review as a whole the underwear women have worn during the past five hundred years. It becomes no more reassuring as examples of actual garments mount up progressively with the approach nearer to our own time. The undress parade zig-zags grotesquely through the centuries and takes a long, long time to reach today and what, not without fears of complacency and arrogance, we regard as being the first-ever exercise of something approaching reason and commonsense on the subject. The future, after all, may decry us as we decry the past.

Viewed from the opening of the 1970's the distortions and discomforts of female underwear of the past seem almost nightmarish, even when we are beguiled by the outer glamour and splendour of those lost ladies of old years in their panniers, crinolines and bustles.

It even seems incredible that until knitted woollen and woven cellular underclothing was introduced in the 1880's not a single undergarment conformed to the natural female shape or even tried to. And that after that, until the 1920's, most underwear was still extraordinarily and inexplicably voluminous. All that bunching and gathering, tucking and frilling—what was the sense of it? Why should chemises and drawers be three times the size of the wearers? Why should layer upon layer of underclothes have been worn?

Apart from the successive psychological and sociological reasons for the oddity in various eras, there is another more immediately disturbing practical consideration. It is that through most of those 500 years, up to the mid 1850's, all these voluminous garments were sewn by hand. Human fingers toiled over yards upon endless yards of minute hemming and other seaming until the introduction of the sewing machine. Even after that hand-made, but not home-made, underwear continued to be in great demand for the better quality market. This lasted until well into the 'twenties of this century and remained a prestige point up to the post-war introduction of nylon as a lingerie material in the late 1940's.

To describe in full the manufacture of underwear through the centuries would be another story and one involving different and complex approaches. But certain aspects of this subject have profoundly affected the undergarments women have worn in successive periods and certain landmarks in the manufacturing story have contributed greatly to the development of such garments.

Sewing was traditionally a 'natural' for the girl or woman who had to support herself or starve—as has been the lot of most of humanity in all ages. 'The needle', says Wanda Fraiken Neff, 'is an even more primitive instrument of women's toil than the spinning-wheel, yet between the days when fishbone, bone, or ivory was used to fashion the skins of animals or rude fabrics into clothing, and the age when the domestic manufacture of steel needles planted in Worcestershire and Warwickshire towns by the Germans was developed into one of the great machine industries, stretched a period of obscurity for the English women who wielded the needle'.

There are references to seamstresses in the literature of the sixteenth and early seventeenth centuries. Jane in Dekker's *Shoemaker's Holiday* (1600) worked in a seamster's shop making 'fine cambricke shirts and bands'. In the mid-seventeenth century there are records of girls being apprenticed as seamstresses for seven years. The terms of their hire are not known, but the system originated with the medieval craft guilds and was codified by Queen Elizabeth into a national policy which protected the craftsmen and his customers from unskilled competitors. It did not fit into factory conditions and at the time of the Industrial Revolution seamstresses emerge as unorganised and subject to deplorable working conditions. When, in the 1830's, agitation arose about legislation to control factory conditions for women, opponents of it produced the callous argument that workers in the cotton mills were no worse off than other working women.

It was a fact that when the Industrial Revolution began the position of women in business and in the labour market in general deteriorated and diminished. This was partly due to the snobbish prestige of the unoccupied woman which attended the increase in middle-class wealth and lasted to a considerable degree until the early part of the twentieth century. It was also caused in part by the reorganisation of labour brought about by new industrial production in factories. Before that, when small businesses predominated, the home was often above the shop or work-place and the women of the household took an active part in many of their husband's or father's affairs. 'In the seventeenth and eighteenth centuries there had been numerous crafts and trades in which women were engaged', records Sir Charles Petrie, 'either on their own account or as married women assisting their husbands. It was still the age of small-scale businesses, and in many trades the skilled worker was both craftsman and merchant, producing goods at home and selling direct to the consumer; such workers, both men and women, formed a considerable section of the shopkeeping classes. Where the workshop was attached to the home it was customary for the whole family to work together in the craft'. This applied widely to the clothing trade, of which underwear and corsetry were considerable parts.

In the middle-class section of society the Victorian trend was to kill the idea of business partnership in marriage and to segregate women into leisure—or idleness—but in the case of the working classes the state of affairs as regards women workers was very different. There were vast numbers of women urgently needing to work in order to live and there were not enough jobs for them, even though the rapid succession of mechanical inventions by people like Hargreaves, Arkwright and Crompton in spinning and by Kay, Stell and Cartwright in weaving created a huge demand for factory labour in the booming home and export textile trade. Most of this was supplied by women and children. By 1884 there were 242,000 women and girls working in cotton mills in Britain, mostly under appalling conditions, often married, with children who in turn went to work at agonisingly early ages.

The census of 1841 showed that the dressmaking and millinery trades—they were closely allied at that time—had more than 106,000 women employed in them. They came from a greater variety of classes and types than the factory workers, and the conditions in which they worked were in many cases far worse than those of factory workers.

In the middle of the nineteenth century milliners and dressmakers often worked from 4 a.m. to 10 p.m. and sometimes till midnight. Most girls came from the country and were apprenticed to the owners of shops in the towns. One estimate gives their expectation of a working life as three or four years, so heavy was the toll on health. The girls came from various classes, from factory

families to well-educated girls of gentle birth. Lord Shaftesbury, the
father of nineteenth-century factory legislation and the instigator
of the series of factory acts which gradually improved the working
conditions of men, women and children, stated that the daughters
of poor clergymen, half-pay officers or tradesmen who had fallen
on hard times took to dressmaking. Fiction of the time tells the same
story. Jane Eyre tried to get work as a dressmaker, then as a plain
sewer and finally as a servant. Maggie Tulliver in *The Mill on the
Floss* said: 'Plain sewing was the only thing I could get money by'.

These dressmakers' apprentices paid a premium of £50 or £60 for
two or three years, during which they received board and lodging
from their employers. Outdoor apprentices, living at home, paid no
premium and were paid no wages. There were endless complaints of
overwork and breakdowns in health and of the fact that girls were
not taught their trade properly but were kept on unskilled plain
work. At the time of the summer and winter London Seasons girls
were found by Government Inspectors in 1843 to be working at
dressmaking from 5 or 6 in the morning until 2 or 3 the next morning with no proper breaks or rest. Widespread similar evidence of
appalling hours and conditions of work was recorded in Parliamentary papers of that year. One witness testified to having worked
from 4 a.m. on Thursday until 10.30 a.m. on the following Sunday
on orders for general mourning for William IV. Another girl
recorded that she had not changed her dress for nine days or nights,
had rested on a mattress on the floor by her work and had her food
cut up and placed beside her so that she could go on sewing while she
ate. Even normally twelve or thirteen hours was the accepted
working day.

It seems reasonable to assume that the more elegant and intimate
items of underwear, such as the elaborate petticoats of the time,
would be made by these skilled girls. Health suffered. Consumption
was rife. Eyesight was impaired. And the villains of the piece were
usually women—women employers and their fashionable women
clients demanding up to date clothes and placing orders as late as
possible so as to be in the very height of fashion.

Plain sewing, which would account for a large proportion of
underwear, was in the main carried out by dressmakers who went
out working for the day or did plain sewing at home as outworkers.
The daily British rate round the middle of the century was 1s. 0d.
or 1s. 6d. Little Dorrit worked in this way. Women who did this

plain sewing at home were generally described as 'slop workers' and were the lowest class of the dressmaking trade. They worked for contractors who paid them the barest minimum and who could return work on the grounds that it was not of a high enough standard. Workers were told to call at a certain hour at the shop employing them in order to collect work and there were frequent complaints that they were kept waiting from an hour up to half a day, with consequent loss of working time. The *Christian Ladies' Magazine* for 1835 stated that a woman who worked from 7 a.m. till midnight might not earn 1s. 6d. a day. A staymaker is quoted as making 2s. 6d. a week — less than a dollar in the currency of the time. The general rates of pay were obtained from Government investigations which showed that in 1843 10d. a dozen was paid for shirt-making. In one establishment employing 1200 to 1400 women pay was from 1s. 6d. to 10s. 6d. a week, with 5s. 6d. as the average. Carlyle in his *Latter Day Pamphlets* wrote of 'this blessed exchange of slop shirts for the souls of women'.

The whole record of the seamstresses is a black one. To sweated labour and oppressive employers there was added competition from the workhouse, where female members employed in sewing and staymaking undercut the independent worker. An array of workhouse corsets of the earlier part of last century is on view in the collection of Richard Coopers of Ashbourne, a famous corset firm of today. *Punch* referred to this unfair competition, and the tragic misery of the slop worker and her plain sewing has been highlighted unforgettably in the stinging lines of the famous poem 'The Song of the Shirt' by Thomas Hood, first published in the Christmas number of *Punch* in 1843.

Attempts to better the position of the women seamstresses were long and difficult. Reformers like Sir Robert Peel in 1844 made slow progress in their attempts to improve the position of such unorganised and desperately poor working women. Lord Shaftesbury's attempted bill of 1855 failed through Government indifference and the vote-catching fact that the rich, voting classes wanted their supply of cheap labour to maintain the world of feminine fashion. As for the oppressed women, there was constant difficulty in obtaining evidence of bad treatment from them because the victims were in fear of their employers and any work was better than none.

Reform of the dressmaking and sewing trades was woefully slow to come. In 1908 girl dressmakers worked on Ascot gowns from 8 one morning until 4 on the following afternoon, with only brief intervals for food and rest. The clothing trade—though one of the largest and most luxurious users of female labour—has a long-standing reputation for bad working conditions and poor wages. To this day rates of payment in it are often low in relation to those of women in industry as a whole.

Relief from the agony of endless hand-stitching did, however, come in the shape of the sewing machine, though, like most mechanical inventions of the kind, it was resisted by the workers concerned. It could sew more quickly, so they thought many of them would be put out of work. They did not foresee the expansion of the demand for clothing. The first use of the sewing machine in Britain was for corsetry, and as a remover of drudgery its effect on underwear has been particularly strong and altogether for the good. Hand made clothing today is practically non-existent, although right up to the late nineteen-twenties the prestige of hand-made lingerie persisted and extended to big stores, where the prices for it were often only a few shillings more than those for a corresponding machine-made garment.

The idea of a machine to do stitching was first conceived by an Englishman, Thomas Saint. In 1790 he was granted a patent on a machine for sewing leather and his drawings of it show certain features essential to the modern sewing machine. He devised the overhanging arm, the up-and-down movement of the needle, the horizontal bed or plate to support the sewing, and also the use of a continuous thread. He appears, however, never to have put his innovation to practical use.

The first man to obtain a patent and exercise his right to it was a poor French tailor, Barthelemy Thimmonier. By 1829 he had mastered the mechanical difficulties and produced a sewing machine which made a chain stitch by means of a hooked needle like a crochet hook. In 1830 he took out his patent, and by 1831 eighty of his machines were making uniforms for the French army. These machines were, however, destroyed by a mob, who, like the Luddites in the case of the spinning jenny and other craftsmen throughout industrial history when confronted by new machines, thought their jobs were being threatened by the mechanical contrivance that did their sewing for them.

Thimmonier went back to his home, but he persevered with his invention. By 1845 he had developed it so far that it could sew two hundred stitches a minute and could be used on all kinds of materials from muslin to leather.

He took out patents in England in 1849, and in the U.S.A. in 1850, but by this time he had missed his big opportunity. Other inventors were in the field with more practical machines. He died in poverty in 1857 at the age of 64.

From England and France the initiative in sewing-machine invention had passed to America, but it took the labours of a generation of inventors there to make the sewing machine a really practical manufacturing device. The first man to produce a sewing machine containing nearly all the essential parts of the best modern machines was an American Quaker, Walter Hunt, who also invented the safety-pin. His was a lock-stitch machine, using an eye-pointed needle which worked in combination with a shuttle carrying a second thread.

In 1838 Hunt suggested to his daughter Caroline that she should start manufacturing corsets on one of his machines, but she was afraid to do so—for the familiar reason that it might put the hand-stitchers out of work and create unrest. Discouraged, Hunt sold out his invention to George Arrowsmith, but it fell into disuse and his machine lay forgotten in a garret for fifteen years.

To Elias Howe must be given credit for setting the sewing machine fair and square on its way to being the accepted means of clothing production of all kinds. He invented a lock-stitch machine and, although he lacked Hunt's original inventive talent, he had persistence and confidence in himself. These were qualities needed for the big drive, now about to start in earnest, to get rid of a centuries-old tradition of slow, laborious hand-sewing and to hand the work over to operators working at sewing machines of ever-increasing speed, versatility and efficiency. Unfortunately, however, Howe did not possess all the organisational qualities needed, and he was not destined to be the man to go the whole way towards securing all-over acceptance of the elusive machine. In 1847 he came from America to England and, after eight months' hard work, adapted his invention to the requirements of a Mr. William Thomas, who manufactured corsets, by hand-labour of course, in his shop in Cheapside. But for some reason this venture did not bring the expected break-through.

Meantime, back in America, several ingenious mechanics who had seen Howe's machine were working on his ideas, involving him in a long series of legal disputes and difficulties.

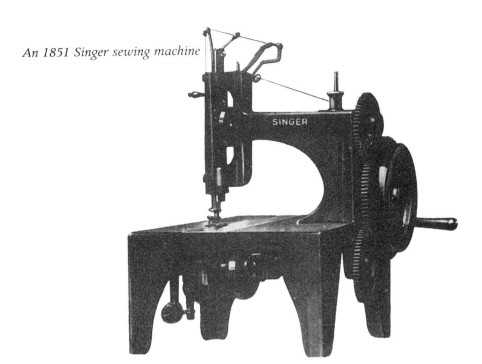

An 1851 Singer sewing machine

The break-through to success was achieved by Isaac Merrit Singer, the first man to produce a practical sewing machine and to bring it into general use, first in America and then in England.

In 1851 Singer developed the idea of the reciprocating shuttle. In addition, he introduced a positive mechanical feed, and the needle bar which had pushed horizontally, was replaced by a straight needle which worked up and down. This was the first lock-stitch machine to do continuous stitching, the lack of which was the biggest defect in the Howe machine. Singer also invented the yielding vertical presser foot to hold the work in place. He first took out a patent for his machine on 12th August 1851, and in that year the firm of I. M. Singer & Co. was established.

The experience of Walter Hunt with the corset trade as an outstanding sphere of usefulness for the sewing machine was repeated by Singer, but this time with happier results. The first sewing machines to be brought into Britain were seen in America in 1855 by Mr. Robert Symington, a young member of the Market Harborough family which had already laid the small foundations of what was to become an immense corset company. Robert Symington did not make the fortune he had hoped for in his impetuous venture to the New World at the age of eighteen, but he brought back something which led the way to fortune at home and was probably in the long

Singer and Wheeler & Wilson sewing machines of the late eighties

run much more valuable. He bought three of the new sewing machines and had them installed in the Market Harborough cottage workroom where corset-making was presided over by his mother. The full story of the consequent rise of the Symington Company is on record and will be told later.

While Singer was trying out his sewing machine, a similar line of experiment, quite unrelated to his, was proceeding in Adrian, Michigan. Here early in 1849 Allen Benjamin Wilson, who had never seen or even heard of the Howe machine, invented a sewing machine.

A Mr. Wheeler saw Wilson's invention in New York, went into partnership with Wilson, and superintended the manufacture of the new machines. Wilson invented the rotary hook and a patent was taken out for this on August 12th 1851 — the same day that Isaac Singer was granted the patent for his first machine. It was a strange coincidence, but one that has many parallels in the course of invention. Wilson also patented the first stationary circular disc bobbin, which was a basic innovation in sewing machine construction. Of all the sewing machine pioneers, Wilson was the most original and many of his devices are still embodied in the machines of today.

The last of the sewing machine pioneers was James Gibbs, from Virginia. His curiosity about machine stitching was roused by seeing a picture in a paper, and then by watching an early Singer machine working in a tailor's shop in 1850. In his view the machine was far too clumsy, complicated and expensive, and he set to work to produce something simpler, cheaper and more practical. His chief

original invention was the chain stitch machine, very much as we
know it today. Gibbs showed his work to James Wilcox, who was so
impressed that he suggested a working partnership. The Wilcox
and Gibbs sewing machine, which was the means of developing
Gibb's ideas, was to play an important part in the subsequent
development of the machine.

It is, incidentally, a curious fact that when it was shown at the
Great Exhibition of 1851 the sewing machine attracted very little
attention. It was not even mentioned in reviews of the Exhibition,
with its enormous presentation of machinery, divided into six
groups and ranging from engineering and building to naval and
military equipment, agricultural machinery and scientific instru-
ments. None the less the sewing machine from this time onwards
came increasingly into use and it was to be largely responsible for an
entirely new conception of clothing, a new era of mass production,
an increasing rapidity in fashion changes and, not least, the development of corsetry and underwear manufacture as a major industry
with a turnover of many millions of pounds a year.

A sewing machine of the late
nineties used especially for the manufacture
of corsets and other women's wear.
It was fitted with from three to twelve
needles, and could carry out parallel rows
of fine lock-stitching

Corsetry manufacture had a story of its own, both in Britain and elsewhere. In France Louis XIV formed a company of dressmakers with the right to make many articles of attire, but the staymakers reserved the right to operate exclusively in their own trade. About 1660, also, certain tailors dedicated themselves expressly to stay-making. They were known as *tailleurs de corps*—the last word was still used in France for the corset until well into the eighteenth century.

In Britain too the staymaker by the eighteen century was a specialist, a highly-regarded individual craftsman making bespoke garments for ladies of fashion. A great many women of more modest pretentions made their corsets at home, and paper patterns of them were supplied in women's magazines, which by that time were numerous, varied, widely read and intent on guiding and advising their readers on all matters from morals to fashion.

For some reason the scene showing the staymaker, a man, fitting a lady with her stays was a favourite subject for illustration by artists. A great number of prints and engravings show this process,

A stay-maker's trade card, 1766

'The Stay-maker' by Hogarth

sometimes elegantly, but more often with an excess of realism and even as grotesque cartoons, with the lady shown as repulsively ugly and old.

Every town had its staymakers and an unusual record of them in London and elsewhere is preserved by a substantial number of their trade cards, now in the Department of Prints and Drawings at the British Museum. These are part of a general collection of trade cards made by Mr. Ambrose Heal and left by him to the Museum. Many of the cards cannot unfortunately be dated, but an early one, about 1730, tells that Henry Gough 'maketh women's stays and children's coats after the newest fashion'. (These two items are frequently paired). Another card, of 1735, belongs to William Mendham who makes 'stays, stomachers, etc. etc.' There is also 'Weatherheads wholesale stomacher warehouse . . . now selling variety of the newest patterns of busk and milboard stomachers on the most reasonable terms'.

There was a depression in the staymaking business when, from about 1800 to 1830, women of fashion took to clinging 'classical' gowns and gave up wearing corsets. But after 1830 fashion reverted to its more elaborate tradition and the staymakers came back into prominence. By this time considerable numbers of women were following this trade, among them being Mrs. Bevern, 'Patent Stay and Corset Maker', of 50 Burlington Street, London. Her card shows a picture of a young lady in the still slim, high waisted dress of the early eighteen-hundreds. S. Gardner, 'French Stay & Corset Maker' of Long Acre, 'where ladies may be fitted with good stays (ready made) from 15s. to 23s', explains on the trade card that 'Mrs. G. is daughter to Mr. Meggitt, Staymaker, Holborn'.

By the 1830's the staymaker was expanding his (or her) business and either had a workroom or employed ten or twelve outworkers. Entry to the craft was by apprenticeship. The staymaker, however, as an independent craftsman did not survive the arrival of the sewing machine and the mechanisation of corset manufacture in factories. He either became absorbed in the new régime or went out of business. The corset trade, however, flourished. The crinoline era gave a great impetus to it and by 1868 British turnover was reckoned at £1,000,000 a year for 3,000,000 corsets. In addition an immense quantity of steel, more than half the whalebone which reached the market, horn, ebonite, wood, gutta percha and hardened brass were also used for stiffening, for busks and for eyelet holes. An additional 2,000,000 corsets were imported each year from France and Germany. A notable manufacturer was De la Garde & Co. of Paris and British customers would send this Company's agent detailed measurements—round the chest below the arms, from beneath the arms to the hips, the circumference of the hips and the waist measure. This meant that 'the fit is a matter of certainty', and British women were enabled to have corsets 'made by the first manufacturers in Europe without the trouble and inconvenience of being attended for the purpose of measurement.' The leading manufacturers in Britain were Messrs. Thomson & Co., who had factories in England, America and the Continent. Their speciality was the glove-fitting corset, ordered by waist measurement only.

During the latter part of the nineteenth century the rising

An 1885 corset advertisement

W. HULL KING & SON'S

HIGH-CLASS

CORSETS

WITHOUT WHICH

THE CELEBRATED

"DUCHESS OF FIFE" CORSET.

Plain Busk. White, 10/6. Black, 12/6.
REAL WHALEBONE

NONE ARE GENUINE.

The special attention of all ladies who are looking for a genuine *Whalebone* Corset at a moderate price is respectfully drawn to this graceful corset. Nothing like it in the trade for fit, comfort, durability, and extreme lowness of price (in real Whalebone) has ever before been shown.

Design and Trade Mark Registered.

OLD STYLE

TRADE **HKS** MARK

(From original picture by OSTADE.)

☞ The Pictorial and Fashion papers having, during recent years, become so full of "Blocks" of the same high-class order, which are used alike for illustrations of the *lowest priced and inferior makes* as well as the best goods, and which are therefore confusing, disappointing, and misleading to Ladies who are in search of a really good Corset, we therefore prefer sending, on application, our Illustrated Catalogue and Price List, containing description and illustrations of all our makes, as well as Press Notices of the same, also name of nearest Draper or Corsetier supplying them will be sent.

Ask for the "W. H. K. & S." Corsets.

To be obtained of the London Agents: Messrs. SHOOLBRED & CO., Tottenham Court-road, W.; WATERLOO HOUSE and SWAN & EDGAR Ltd., Regent-street, W.; Messrs. CAPPER, SON, & CO., Ltd., 63 & 64, Gracechurch-street, E.C.; PETER ROBINSON, Oxford-street, W.; Messrs. GREEN & EDWARDS, Circus-road, St. John's Wood; and all first-class Drapers and Staymakers everywhere.

NEW STYLE

GUARANTEED WHALEBONE

THE "DUCHESS OF FIFE" CORSET.

NO satisfactory substitute has ever been found for BEST WHALEBONE, which defies any imitation and comes triumphantly through the severest test.

Send for Illustrated Price List of these and other Corsets.

Wholesale: 35, PERCY ST., RATHBONE PLACE, LONDON, W.

An advertisement from 'Fashions of Today', 1894

interest in the construction of corsetry is shown by the fact that between 1800 and 1850 only seventeen patents were taken out in the corset trade. But from 1867 to 1900 five hundred were granted. Most of them applied to small details, but they indicated that women felt strongly about having corsets with something special about them.

By a happy chance there exists a detailed first-hand record of the complete change-over from an old-style cottage workroom, run by a staymaker of great skill and ability in the first half of last century, to a world-famous foundationwear company. This record exists in a centenary commemorative history, *In Our Fashion,* produced privately in 1956 by Symingtons of Market Harborough, a family which last century became a household name in such diverse spheres as grocery, food manufacture and corsetry.

Between 1827 and 1840 three brothers, William, James and Samuel Symington left their home at Leadhills, Lanarkshire, and came one by one to Market Harborough to set up in business. James opened a shop as a tailor, hatter and woollen merchant. In 1832 the house next to where he lived was taken over by a family named Gold, whose daughter Sarah had learned from her mother the skilled craft of staymaking, at that time a matter of apprenticeship. This involved the making of beautifully finished garments, with rows of narrow whalebones stitched into them by hand and often with decorative embroidery in contrasting colours.

In 1835 James and Sarah were married and Sarah evidently continued her trade of staymaker. She had nine children, but did not let her career lapse. In a bill heading of 1842 James describes himself as 'linen and woollen draper, hatter, hosier and staymaker'.

These were days of intensifying tight-lacing and Sarah Symington became increasingly well-known for her skill. By 1850 a cottage in a yard off the High Street was leased as the first Symington workroom and soon afterwards an adjacent double-fronted shop was added. Sarah started with three girls and work went on from six in the morning until ten at night on the fine sewing and embroidery required for corsets for the local gentry of prosperous Leicestershire. There was neither gas nor water in the premises and, with the Window Tax still in force, little light either, but such working conditions, strange as it seems, were still taken for granted at that time.

In 1855 Robert Symington, James and Sarah's eldest son, then only in his eighteenth year, decided to seek his fortune in America

and it was he who came back within a year, not with a fortune but with three Singer sewing machines. His mother was an enthusiastic convert, but the girls, now six in all, refused to work 'the devilish American contraption which had to be treadled from a standing position like the old street knife grinders and which was so obviously designed to throw seamstresses out of work'.

Sarah Symington, however, won over the girls and, as a result of the growth of her business, Symingtons, one of the first mechanised corset factories in England, was established in 1856. Output rose, prices fell, business expanded. The factory and production grew by means of additional premises, increased labour and the recruitment of outworkers from several surrounding villages. Outwork stations, supplied by horse and van from Market Harborough, were maintained for this purpose. During the next quarter of a century there was no end to the expansion of the business. The labour force rose to over 1000 and outworkers poured into the Market Harborough headquarters often with children and always with prams, to take away loads of corsets to be corded at home. The labour position at this period was that girls from what was called the labouring class could either enter domestic service or work in a factory. Symingtons had a reputation for good working conditions—clean, light and, by Victorian standards, spacious and well lit. But hours were appallingly long. Girls had to be at the factory at 6 a.m. There was a breakfast break at 7.30., which usually meant a scamper home and back within half an hour. The day did not end till between 6 and 8 in the evening. Work went on on Saturday mornings.

Although recorded as excellent employers, competing successfully in the demand for workers which prevailed all over the neighbourhood, Symingtons did not question the fairness of these hours. Discipline was severe, but when, in the 1870's, an outstanding young woman member of the Symington family, Miss Perry Gold Symington, took the then exceptional step of abandoning ladylike leisure and going into the business as what we would today call personnel officer, even she did not question the system. She regarded the employees with affection and made their welfare her responsibility, but Victorian ideas of working hours were still unquestioned.

Apart from the general progress made in factory conditions and wages in this century, and an enormous increase in demand due to vastly improved standards of living, the main influence on underwear in recent years is that, even more than outerwear, it has become classless. In the later nineteenth century it was the supreme example of class distinction in dress. A whole world divided the silk and satin, lace and ribbon, frou-frous and frills of the rich from the rough cotton and flannel of the poor. But today the Colonel's lady and Judy O'Grady are sisters immediately under their dresses more than anywhere else.

A 1913 advertisement

LONGFELLOW'S immortal poem "EXCELSIOR" and the "EXCELSIOR" CORSETS have many points in common. Both are products of artists at the top of the profession, and on their distinctive merits cannot be excelled.

EXCELSIOR
CORSETS
ARE THE BEST
VALUE

on the market to-day, and the Draper who does not stock them is neglecting his own interests.

14/11 per doz. **17/11** per doz. **22/11** per doz.

The "Excelsior" Showcard now being distributed is invaluable for artistic Window Display, giving a distinction not attainable with ordinary Showcards.

EXCELSIOR CORSETS
are manufactured by the makers of the

Qual. A.
14/11 per doz.

FAMOUS **DOUBLE AXE BRAND** CORSETS.

Trade Mark

An advertisement of the 1920's

The Gossard *Line of Beauty*

While it is true that the prevailing cult of the slender line silhouette makes the largest demand on the resources of the Gossard factory, it is the proud boast of the Gossard organisation that their extensive range of models are individually designed to meet the correct figure needs of every type. And such is the care exercised by the distributors of Gossard foundation garments that you may rely upon a fitting that might have been expressly designed and tailored for you. The fashionable hostess, the sports girl, the business woman, the matron and the maid—for each and all Gossard foundation garments are specially designed.

<table>
<tr><td>MODEL 1872.</td><td>MODEL 543</td></tr>
<tr><td>This Combination is particularly suited to medium and large figures desiring a lightweight garment, because of the uplift, satin tricot top, and the freedom offered by the elastic inserts at the side and lower front.
Sizes 32 to 40 - - 12/6</td><td>This popular step-in is made of brocade, with elastic sections, at each side. Elastic inserts are also placed at each side of the centre front, permitting free movement, and perfect anchorage of the garment.
Sizes 26 to 34 - - 26/6</td></tr>
</table>

We will gladly send you free, on application, a copy of our New Season's Art Catalogue, together with name of nearest Gossard distributor.

Your Gossard Corsetière will be glad to show you a selection of new Gossard Completes, Clasp-arounds, Combinations, Step-ins, and Front Lacing Corsets.

THE BRITISH H. W. GOSSARD CO. LTD.

(Wholesale only.)

This change became noticeable after the 1914–18 war. Referring to this period Goronwy Rees, in his *History of Marks & Spencer*, suggests: 'One might perhaps say that the discarding of the steel or whalebone corset, the flannel petticoat, in favour of a webbed elastic girdle and cotton or artificial silk underclothing did more for women's emancipation than the vote. But the war also raised women's social and economic prestige by turning her into a wage-earner. She became an important economic factor both as a producer and a consumer'.

There is more than a process of social and sociological change in this. Underwear, as has been shown, has proved particularly susceptible to the virtues of man-made fibres and of new, constantly-developing methods of mass production. As these fabrics emerged an increasing proportion of underwear began to be made from them by large organisations and to be sold under nationally

An advertisement of the mid twenties

A 1930 advertisement

well-known brand names. A very big share of the market came into the orbit of the chain stores and this trend has been increasing in recent years.

The largest of all the British manufacturing and retail sources of underwear today is Marks & Spencer. They now manufacture at least two-fifths of all the briefs worn by British women and about a quarter of their entire lingerie. They also produce approximately a third of all types of bras and over a quarter of all corsets (including pantee-girdles and all other types of foundations). This compares with the fact that in clothing generally the Company's total sales of £255,000,000 in 1969 accounted for between ten and eleven per cent of British expenditure on clothes. This immense output is absorbed by all classes. The same garments are bought and worn by duchess and deb, career woman and trend-setter.

Marks & Spencer's progress in underwear corresponds closely to the development of the new fabrics. They first entered the field in 1929, when they launched lock-knit rayon, or artificial silk knickers which sold at 1s. 0d. a pair. They were prosaic garments in the then prevalent style, knee-length and rather voluminous, with elastic at the waist and legs. Rayon was the only synthetic material used by them until 1947. This was the year when nylon began to be more freely available for civilian use, and Marks & Spencer launched into it with fancy mesh warp-knitted nylon, which became the real basis of their future vast output of nylon underwear. Surprisingly, the slip they made sold at 23s. 11d., with briefs at 9s. 11d. and a night-dress at 29s. 11d. These prices were to be reduced considerably as the market expanded and in the case of briefs in particular they were to be slashed.

For some time rayon and nylon sold side by side, but rayon gradually gave way to newer synthetics and by 1957 nylon was the principal lingerie fabric in the Company's range—and in the market generally. It still remains so. In that year, too, Marks & Spencer made two other important moves. They had for many years had a policy of laying down specifications for garment make-up, but now they went further. There were many different types and weights of nylon being offered. Steps were taken by their technologists to establish a suitable standard of quality of this successful man-made fibre, in conjunction with the nylon producer, the knitter and, of course, the manufacturer making up the fabric into lingerie. They also introduced 15 denier nylon for semi-transparent slips and nightdresses, making these garments, in bright colours instead of the pastels that had prevailed until then. This move was a fantastic success.

Prices came down substantially by 1961, thanks to increased output. In recent years there has been a consolidation of a fashion policy of continually introducing new materials, designs, ideas. Today's lingerie doesn't wear out, so variety is the key to maintaining sales. In the last five or six years Terylene and Dacron have been used to an increasing extent. Today fine shirt fabrics are going into slips. Crepon nylon and crepe nylon are also taking part in a move towards the use of more woven fabrics.

The large-scale introduction in 1966 of the bra slip, probably the greatest innovation in underwear in recent years, was instigated by Marks & Spencer when the idea was almost confined to French boutiques. It found immediate acceptance, soon became the biggest fashion development of the Company and today commands about fifty per cent of total sales of this garment.

As underwear is showing no divergence from its present functional character, it is likely that mass production will continue to be responsible for a major part of it. It is improbable that here there will be any of the extraordinary 'revivals' that have beset the recent course of outer fashion. Underwear seems to be soundly based on the needs of the human body, and, whether plain or fancy, it is always expected to be lightweight, free from bulk, comfortable, drip-dry and non-iron. As such it continues to progress. The man-made fabrics used for it are becoming more and more interesting and varied. Styles are currently becoming increasingly feminine, indicating that, though the world around us is changing, human nature remains much the same. In the immediate future there could well be an extension of the 1970 swing-back to femininity, with, inevitably, increasingly attractive underwear.

What lies further ahead for fashion, and therefore for underwear, is impossible to predict. James Laver considers that 'we are on the eve of a social revolution the magnitude of which is only just beginning to be understood'. In the long view it is scarcely conceivable that the fashions of the future should resemble those of the past or follow any familiar cycle. The breakaway from tradition is already under way; Unisex clothes have put men and women into almost identical trousers and identical shirts and pullovers, with, underneath, almost identical briefs (only the bra survives from the past!). Nothing like this has ever happened before in the history of fashion.

Other present-day signs of change are even more unprecedented, though up to now they have had little or no practical effect on clothing. Are we dealing with outerwear or underwear or an amalgam of both when confronted with such recent freak fashions as bras made of solid metal discs and dresses composed of linked squares or circles of brass, chromium or plastic? Can we deny that space suits for travellers could be a commercially viable range of clothing within the lifetime of our children? Could corsets and bras be sprayed on each morning and washed off at night?

In addition to undreamed-of fibres and fabrics from the laboratory, new processes of manufacture will almost certainly be introduced. Already high-frequency welding has replaced sewing for certain types of garments, but foundations and underwear are likely to be less adaptable to this process than raincoats and overalls. Welding is, however, a top talking point in present-day speculation on the future of clothing and underwear, because it would mean a revolution in production and a large-scale displacement of machinists. Against its early development in foundationwear and underwear is the fact that the costly equipment required would have to be adapted to the different weights and thicknesses of material which are very frequent in these categories of clothing. This would be very expensive. In addition, very long runs are necessary if welding is to be profitable and this would lead to too great a degree of standardisation of design. It might be used for main seams but, on present showing, is unlikely in the near future to be applicable to the many details of women's foundationwear and underwear manufacture. Moulding is another possibility. It is already being used for bra cups and could possibly be extended to some foundationwear. The idea of a tube that can build shape into a product has already been applied to stockings and tights and could well be extended to other items of women's wear.

Disposable underwear is another portent of the future. Packets of panties made of paper or rayon have already secured a place in shops and chain stores. Inflammability and the price factor have up to now limited the production of other garments in similar materials, but the possibility of disposable clothing becoming generally accepted is far from fantasy. If it came, would there be any likelihood of survival for the traditional division of clothing into outer and under?

It could well be that the story of fashion as it has developed during the past five hundred years would come to an end and be just another subject for the antiquarians to study. But, meantime, the women of Britain spend more than £900,000,000 a year on clothing and of that total nearly a tenth goes on foundations and more on other underwear. Fashion is still big business, as well as living history, and underwear is an essential part of it.

Bibliography

Allen, Agnes, *The Story of Clothes*, Faber & Faber, 1955; Roy
   Publishers, New York

Arnold, Janet, *Patterns of Fashion 1680–1860,* Wace & Co. Ltd,
   1964

Ashdown, Mrs Charles, *British Costume During XIX Centuries,*
   Thomas Nelson & Sons Ltd, 1953

Bradfield, Nancy, *Costume in Detail 1730–1930,* Harrap, 1968

Brooke, Iris, *A History of English Costume,* Methuen, 1937; Theatre
   Arts Books, New York

Buck, Anne, *Victorian Costume & Costume Accessories,* Herbert
   Jenkins, 1961; Universe Books, New York
   Corsetry & Underwear, Circle Publications, 1935–1970

Cunnington, C. Willett and Phillis, *History of Underclothes,* Michael
   Joseph, 1951

Cunnington, Phillis and Mansfield, Alan, *English Costume for Sports
   and Outdoor Recreation. From the 16th to the 19th centuries,*
   A. & C. Black, 1969; Barnes & Noble, Inc., New York

Dunbar, Janet, *The Early Victorian Woman,* G. G. Harrap, 1955

Evans, Dr. Joan, *Dress in Medieval France,* Oxford University Press,
   1952

Garland, Madge, *Fashion,* Penguin Books, 1962

Gibbs-Smith, Charles H., *The Fashionable Lady in the 19th Century,*
   H.M. Stationery Office, 1960; British Information Services,
   New York

Jaeger, Gustav, *Health Culture,* translated by Lewis R. S. Tomalin,
   new revised edition, Dr Jaeger's Sanitary Woollen System Co.
   Ltd, 1907

Laver, James, *Fashion,* Cassell, 1963

Laver, James, *Concise History of Costume,* Thames & Hudson, 1969;
   Harry N. Abrams, New York

Laver, James, *Modesty in Dress,* Heinemann, 1969; Houghton
   Mifflin, Boston

Libron F. and Clouzot H., *Le Corset dans l'art et les moeurs du XIIIe
   au XXe siecles,* Paris, 1933

Limner, Luke (John Leighton), *Madre Natura versus the Moloch of*

Fashion, Chatto & Windus, 1874

Lord, William Barry, *The Corset and the Crinoline*, Ward Lock & Tyler, 1868

Neff, Wanda Fraiken, *Victorian Working Women*, George Allen and Unwin, 1929; AMS Press, New York

Petrie, Sir Charles, *Great Beginnings in the Age of Queen Victoria*, Macmillan, 1967

Quennell, Peter, *Victorian Panorama*, Batsford, 1937

Rees, Goronwy, *St. Michael. A History of Marks & Spencer*, Weidenfeld & Nicolson, 1969

St. Laurent, Cecil, *The History of Ladies' Underwear*, Michael Joseph, 1968

Staniland, Kay, *The Medieval Corset. Costume Vol. 3*, Costume Society, 1969

Strachey, Ray, *The Cause*, G. Bell, 1928; Kennikat Press, Port Washington, N.Y.
In Our Own Fashion, Harley Publishing Company, 1956

Taylor, John, *It's a Small, Medium and Outsize World*, Hugh Evelyn, 1966

Waugh, Norah, *Corsets & Crinolines*, Batsford, 1954; Theatre Arts Books, New York

White, Cynthia L., *Women's Magazine 1693–1968*, Michael Joseph, 1970

Index